Harvesting History: While Farming the Flats

"*Harvesting History: While Farming the Flats* is an invitation to sit down in Aggie's farmhouse kitchen as shared memories of country life unfurl like petals from the old roses at the center of the wooden table."

—**Eleanor Coppola, artist, writer and filmmaker**

"Blueberries, blackberries and watercress...Francis, George and Phil. Here are recipes, picture-making anecdotes, and an everlasting respect for soil and water, the light and the rain, the unique husbandry that has existed in Bolinas and West Marin. Aggie Murch has written a wondrous book about the lives that backed up the making of *The Godfather, Apocalypse Now, The Black Stallion* and *The Unbearable Lightness of Being*. It's a reverie on fruits and vegetables, the cats, the horses and the birds, and the artists. And it is a classic straightaway, for while it is plainly honest and factual, it is the evocation of an ordinary paradise, like a great children's book, so that you will wish you had been there—even if you were."

—**David Thomson, author, film historian, and critic**

"This book is like its author: smart, funny, generous, and honest. It is a pure delight to read!"

—**Linda Ronstadt, artist, singer, musician, and writer**

"A delicious memoir of two dissimilar but congruent family paths, farming and film making, and a woman's poetic sensibility bringing them together. A paean to the pastoral life, a small town's closeness, kindnesses, shortcomings and griefs. Throughout is a life richly lived, and beautifully written, a life alongside people and nature in their respective complexity."

—Warren Weber, founding owner farmer of the oldest continuously certified organic farm in California

"Blackberry Farm is Aggie Murch's *Walden Pond*. She made existence sustainable, rebuilt life over and over, helped spirits enter the world and gently helped them leave. She's got the gift: she's both Nature and Nurture, all in one package. I look upon her as Aggie the Invincible, Wondrous Woman. Be great if those Guys Down There could figure out some way of making a franchise out of a woman like her. I'd vote to see that movie. And wouldn't we all be better off."

—Philip Kaufman, film director and screenwriter

"What a ride! Aggie Murch's memoir afforded me the opportunity to explore hidden rooms of my own life that I didn't even know were there; or had forgotten, or that just needed to be prompted back into consciousness. Weaving together agriculture and Hollywood, Bolinas and Britain, she chronicles food, film, farming, family and friends in a way that is neither contradictory nor self-proclaiming."

—Orville Schell, journalist and author of *The Town That Fought to Save Itself,* Arthur Ross Director of Center on US-China Relations, Asia Society

"I dare you to read Aggie Murch's generous, charming memoir and not wish you had her as a best friend. She writes stunningly and enthusiastically about raising children, horses, a garden of rare roses, free-range chickens, and old rare apples without ever becoming too sentimental. She finds time to listen to friends, notice her first red-tailed hawk, ride her horse Babe, and cook tasty meals from her garden and from the sea that laps close to her land. The appealingly unfussy recipes that are included are a result of her British background and an assumed Western point of view—all can feed a family or an army of friends."

—**Peggy Knickerbocker, chef and author**

"Aggie plants you firmly in a place of beauty while at a time of growth and unbridled creativity. Tall and confident, she is woman at ease whether rubbing elbows with film giants, tending to her gentle Italian bees, or adventuring o'er hill and dale with her beloved horse Babe. A tea-powered force of nature, this nurturing mother and loving wife endows the reader with delectable chapters of rejuvenating imagery. Paragraphs born of rich Earthy compost, sentences tilled from decades of experience, her words are harvested, each bringing a lifetime of experience to the reader's plate. With parchment and pen, Aggie heightens our senses, teasing forth the feelings and memories that embrace us with the comfort of rhubarb and custard, the momentary sting of nettle, the chatter and commotion of swallows' spring arrival, or the smell of equine sweat."

—**Keith Hansen, naturalist, visual artist, and author**

"A farmer hears the rain and she pictures the creek "waking up," the water-fueled nutrients rising up into the fresh watercress, "tough yet delicate, like a seasoned character actor." This gripping memoir rests at the intersection of the birth of the independent film movement and the organic farming movement, both in California in the early 1970s. And through such delicately woven metaphors we come to understand this rich and varied life. Muriel "Aggie" Murch is a Karen Blixen-like figure, truly the "returning" woman, as one minute she's jetting to the side of her husband for a movie premier, and the next she is again drawn back to the land, and to the miracle of growth and soil that is the taut thread running through this memoir."

—Gail Reitano, author of *Italian Love Cake: A Novel*

"Aggie Murch warmly takes the reader by the hand and, with charm and humor, leads us through the daily challenges and adventures of motherhood, farming, gardening, and much more. A deeply enjoyable read."

—Nicolette Hahn Niman rancher, lawyer, author

Harvesting History

While Farming the Flats

A Memoir

Muriel A. Murch

Sibylline
DIGITAL FIRST

Published in the United States by Sibylline Press,
an imprint of All Things Book LLC, California.

Sibylline Press is dedicated to publishing the
brilliant work of women authors ages 50 and older.
www.sibyllinepress.com

Sibylline Digital First Edition
eBook ISBN: 9781960573544
Print ISBN: 9781960573698

Cover Design: Alicia Feltman
Book Production: Sang Kim and Aaron Laughlin

**Sibylline
Press**

This book is my answer.
For Carrie A.
Christina B.
Ellie C.
Marcia D.
Janet R.
And all.

MAP OF THE FLATS BY LAURIE M SAWYER, 2024

Prologue

After my husband delivered a lecture to a group of Danish filmmakers and students, Philip calls out, "The last question please," and a young man stands up.

"Mr. Murch, with your work schedule and the traveling, how do you manage a home life?" Then he sits down.

Suddenly, there is a deeper quiet in the room. Philip nods and raises his eyebrows, which always look striking with his large, round, smooth bald head. He nods as if to say, yes, this is a good question, and looks over at Walter.

Walter pauses, not rushing, as he can, to answer with overflowing ideas. Then he responded.

"Truth be told, I don't. I am often on a project for a year, maybe longer, sometimes eighteen months, even two years—and in that time, I may not know where I will be six weeks ahead. You will have to ask Aggie that question."

He smiles and looks up briefly before Philip calls out, "Lunch. We will reconvene in an hour."

"*The soil is the great connector of lives, the source and destination of all. It is the healer and restorer and resurrector, by which disease passes into health, age into youth, death into life. Without proper care for it we can have no community, because without proper care for it we can have no life.*"

—Wendell Berry

Wild Apple Harvest: finding old apples.

Introduction

Migration, moving from one home to another, is sometimes voluntary and sometimes forced. Quite often, we don't know where home is until we are there.

Orville Schell was at the University of California in Berkeley when the San Francisco oil spill occurred in January of 1971. He was already writing about—and involved in—the anti-Vietnam War activism that was brewing and overflowing from the Berkeley campus. But for a while he also became a farmer, plunging into a twenty-year business and ideological partnership with Bill Niman, founder of Niman Ranch, Bolinas, and now owner of the BN Ranch. In 1976, Orville wrote *The Town that Fought to Save Itself*, illustrated with photographs by Ilka Hartman. It was immediately popular, and today remains a classic text on the evolution of a small town, Bolinas, trying to protect itself against America's juggernaut of real estate speculation. Since then, Schell's writings on farming, politics and China have been prolific.

While the working title for this book was *Farming the Flats in a Town that Farmed to Save Itself*, I wrote to Orville, letting him know that I was tipping my hat in his direction. He quickly wrote a kind reply: "Your book sounds like a sweet next chapter in Bolinas's odyssey to wherever it (and all the rest of us!) are going." I realize that going forward from Orville's last page, I too have been looking back, as our town's history is much of my harvest but not all, for our family, farm, and work are woven into and around those memories.

It is in thinking about wherever this town is going and where it has come from that has, in part, prompted this manuscript. Another chapter in the history of our town could be of interest for those who follow along, searching for what they hope to find, a place to be, for it is often still the American way to come from somewhere other. We are all immigrants in our own place and time. Like year-old steers pushed out from the cattle herd, we must make our way, forming new herds of our own. I see our generation as a planked swinging bridge between one dream of America and another, and am ever mindful that we are all stepping stones, one laid down before the other, helping us all to cross the rivers of our lives.

The Town that Fought to Save Itself resonated with the times. During the late 1960s and early '70s, Bolinas was fighting to save itself from what was still accepted by most of the country as the American Dream. In the early 1960s, plans were well under way to develop the hillsides that fanned out below Mount Tamalpais on the northern side of the Golden Gate Bridge. The coastal areas of Bolinas and Stinson Beach were primed to become a Marina Del Rey North, with freeways along the Bolinas Ridge and a helipad on a dredged and yacht-filled lagoon. Led by California Representative Phillip Burton, visionaries, academics, and artists worked together to curb the sprawling runaway development, and helped create the Golden Gate National Recreation Area in 1972. Their political and environmental groundwork in Marin County pushed outward in California's Bay Area at that time and remains a touchstone and inspiration to people in pockets of America and other countries who look to maintain or create integrated agricultural communities. Many in our small township, whose population was made up of farmers, retiring old-timers, and store owners, with just a smattering of vacationing holiday visitors, struggled to adjust to this new energy. Some managed with foresight and grace; others had a harder time of it.

Today, thanks to the teachings and writings of Edward Abbey, Wendell Berry, and, in great part, to the work of Orville Schell, Bill Niman, and Warren Weber—a co-founder of Marin Organic and owner of Star Route Farms, the oldest certified organic farm in Bolinas—the seeds planted in minds and worked into the hard political and physical soil of West Marin have turned over the American sod, exposing the early knowledge of those first Spanish, Swiss, Portuguese, and Italian farmers who came to West Marin in the nineteenth century. To farm in a mindful way, returning organic nutrients to the soil rather than killing it with America's overstocked war chemicals, was a return to an older way and was seen as a renewal of the land. Sustainable farming practices became a defiant act against American agribusiness.

The town of Orville's book has now become *a* town, one of many, and in the intervening fifty years, much has changed: There is a growing movement in towns, villages, and communities in California, in the US, and around the world to reclaim the balance between how we live and how we work on our planet. Bolinas may have been one of the first, but it is not the only place where young, energetic, and determined farmers are reclaiming American land, from the rural East Coast to the Midwest, to even the scarred hills of Kentucky and West Virginia. Admittedly, it is often land that corporations have strip-mined raw for minerals and coal and then abandoned, but still, acre by acre, the soil is recovering its soul.

Generations of farmers have settled in our community and West Marin. Many have persevered, while further north, farmlands slipped into much-needed housing or desired real estate. There are farmers in our community I have barely mentioned, whose work exists but who I don't see from my bistro table tucked away by the window in our farmhouse dining room. This little book could have been written from the other end of Gospel Flats, Paradise Valley, or The Big Mesa; within the Tacherra Ranch, the BN Ranch, Commonweal's Regenerative Design Institute, or downtown, where the amazing pairing of Jeff Creque and Mike Aiken produced the Resource Recovery Center. Among the pioneers who speak out, we can count many from this hamlet and the Bay Area: Angelo Garro, Davia Nelson, Nicolette Hahn Niman, Michael Pollan, and Alice Waters. We are now the old-timers with many tales, memories, and some wisdom. We have been joined by a new generation of young farmers also eager to live on, work, and maybe ask forgiveness from the land, tilling the waft of the soil and blending it into the fabric of community. They are a welcome sight with their energy as they find a way forward, caring for the soil. The struggle reemerges and remains political as we try to "live simply so that others may simply live."

This manuscript began as a fifteen-month journal, starting in 2013 and ending sometime in 2015, of rural life at our home, Blackberry Farm. But the rest of it came from the need to record, to remember, and to share the history of life unfolding in a small and unique geographic space. And so came essays about the land and community, as well as blending in the husband filmmaker. The mixed memories of family, farm, and film from when we grew, alongside our children, on Blackberry Farm, all called out, jostling for their place on the page. With all that jostling, some stories and memories got pushy, some sneaky, creeping into a paragraph here or a page there. They rejected the and-then-this-happened format, each one arriving like schoolchildren in a new classroom, wanting to be beside this other story or that one. While listening to their clamoring, I've arranged them into *their* order, scrambling to pay attention to where we were, and now are, in time and place.

In every barn and farm kitchen, on all small family farms around the world, these stories are repeated. There is laughter and head-shaking sorrow found and remembered. The men and women of the families who came before us have, by their example and interactions, helped shape our lives here. Recording and acknowledging their history from my limited perspective was something I needed to learn and absorb, in order to understand the price of living on this land.

Other influences, like May Sarton's *Life at 70, Journal of a Solitude,* and *Life at 80* have been both encouraging and soothing for me. And then Isak Dinesen's *Out of Africa.* How could one not aspire to, and fall short of, such writing and such heartache? I love our small farm with a passion. It has been our bedrock. We raised our children, our barn, and our greenhouse, and lived out most of our adult lives within its windswept acres. We are grateful that when the outside world has tried to beat us down, the farm held us steady and strong as it did for the Smith and Peters families before us.

★ ★ ★

Because of the different and combined passions and energies Walter and I have shared along our life's path, I have not always been a good partner to the land. The seasons for farming and filmmaking have different rhythms, and it is rare that they begin or end on the same note. Both in film and on the farm, there have been some successes and as many failures. We raised four children, planted many trees, grew countless vegetables, and buried a stable full of equines and other creatures. But I am not the gal I was at age thirty, pounding in fence posts, herding up stray steers, planting apple trees, and guarding my beloved chickens, all in one day.

With the constant encouragement and persistent persuasion of Steve Wax, who extracted this story and that, the farm journal I began has grown into something more. There are memories that are far from the soil I tried to nourish, but in their way, all contribute to its care.

Though completed in Covid times both in London and Bolinas, *Harvesting History While Farming the Flats* remains the notebook jottings of a wife, mother, nurse, and farmer, sitting at the bistro table with her memories. The little table, often bathed in sunlight as I scribbled and looked out at the plum tree, the greenhouse, and a bright yellow beehive, has given way to an all-purpose kitchen, dining, and writing table. In London, the glass door to the terrace is often open to allow visiting cats, foxes, pigeons, and a solitary robin to wander in. The foxes, Lucy and Luke, mostly sunbathe outside. The squirrels continue to try to steal seed from the bird feeder, and the small city birds flit and feed at will. The rhythm is the same at both tables.

Memories get muddled and tangled like kitten-found yarn. There may be errors of memory and perception, and some readers may remember this-as-that or that-as-this. Dates and times might shift, but the names remain our names. The people who were, the people we are, the families we created, are here. Our children, the town's children, may roll their eyes and groan, but then—they may not. Carrie and Connie came to live with us in 1974, joining Walter the Younger (TY) and Beatrice, bringing their friends along with them. Now they all in turn bring their families to the farm that Walter TY and his wife, Sirima Sataman, work hard to hold steady. And with that, more memories are made. It is past time to hand over my shovel and shears and sit back to watch the young birds in the old trees, and the bees hovering over and into new blossoms. I look out at the world beyond in gratitude, and bow my head to memory.

Chapter 1

Copenhagen Calling 2012

I am ready—eager, even—to visit Denmark. It is early December and we will be reunited with our friends Hans-Erik Philip (known as Philip) and his wife, Vibeke Gad. It will be like old times, except that it will be the next generation of young film-makers who stay up well into the dawn mornings, drinking and discussing the day's lectures.

The evening of our arrival, Walter and I meet at the hotel in Copenhagen, each at different stages of jet lag and preparedness. Walter is changing gears, from editing *Particle Fever* in New York to teaching. I have wrapped up a really good apple cider pressing on the farm. I have also brought the first bound draft of short stories that will become *The Bell Lap*. It will remain unopened. We are both exhausted.

The delicate yet hearty Scandinavian hotel breakfast smorgasbord is a treat and, tired as we still are, always worth getting up for. The coffee is strong but not harsh. The breads are fresh, and as they crumble through the cutting boards, they seem to ask, "Toast me or toast me not?" Danish cheeses complement the eggs, fish, and cold meats. Granolas are fresh and barely sweetened, and the off-season fruit is chosen with care. It is a time to linger, even as the businessmen and lecturers reluctantly take their last gulp of coffee, hopefully wiping the stray bread-crumbs from their faces, and rise from their tables.

Philip comes for Walter and they leave for the film school. By the time I arrive, the morning lecture is in full swing. Walter is flanked by Philip and another teacher from the school, and he is revving into fourth gear. The audience is listening eagerly. He has captured them all, and he doesn't miss a beat to acknowledge, or maybe notice, that I have arrived. I find a seat at the end of a row and look around at who has come to this seminar. There is the usual mixture of film students, professors, and professional working men and women. There are picture and sound editors, sound recordists and mixers, directors, and composers. Some are young, maybe with families already; others are older, seasoned in their craft. Like all Scandinavian and European artists, they are keen to hear another talk and explore the growing possibilities of their profession.

The lecture comes to a pause and there is time for a few questions, which Philip deftly fields.

"The last question, please," he asks and a young man stands up.

"Mr. Murch, with your work schedule and the traveling how do you manage a home life?" and he sits down. Suddenly there is a deeper quiet in the room. Philip nods and raises his eyebrows, which always look striking with his large, round, smooth, bald head. He nods as if to say, "Yes, this is a good question," and looks over at Walter. As a composer, teacher, and father, Philip knows this question deserves an answer. Walter has paused too, not rushing, as he can, to answer with overflowing ideas and then he responds.

"Truth be told, I don't. I am often on a project for a year, maybe longer, sometimes eighteen months, even two years—and in that time, I may not know where I will be six weeks ahead. You will have to ask Aggie that question."

He smiles and looks up briefly before Philip calls, "Lunch. We will reconvene in an hour."

There is a quick shuffling all around me as people get up and make their way to the food tables that line the back of the hall. Walter and Philip have disappeared with a couple of other participants who are eager to talk. Vibeke has not arrived and I am slow to move or think about food. Sara Fgaier, Walter's protégée from the Rolex Arts Initiative program, has flown in from Rome to join the seminar for the weekend and has found fellow editors and an old friend with whom to connect. I have only just finished breakfast and go outside to sit alone in a cold wood-fenced courtyard and think about the question posed by that young editor. He looked young, yet old enough to have a family. I didn't have the answer to his question, and up to now had barely thought of it. The reflections and memories that will eventually come to me have not yet arrived.

★ ★ ★

The two-day conference ends and we pack up our bags and my unread *The Bell Lap*. Our flight leaves in the evening and so we are able to visit with Philip and Vibeke, who have planned an adventure for us. Vibeke wants me to see the Karen Blixen Museum in Rungstedlund and Philip has another museum in mind for Walter. It is a clear winter's day in Denmark, and, as Philip drives along the coast, we relax, even as the cold from the sea creeps into the car. But the sun is out and the northern light gives us a view of the Oresund Strait; dimly, in the distance, we can see Sweden. Maybe it is the cold and harsh light that makes me feel the Earth's horizon.

The Rungstedlund estate sits on forty-five acres of land, dedicated to Karen Blixen's place in the pantheon of Danish and world literature. We pull into the gravel driveway, which crunches under the car tires when we stop. Though it is a Monday, when the museum is usually closed, Philip has phoned ahead and made arrangements, so a pale, fair-haired young woman is there to welcome us. She opens the door into the house, leads us in and then leaves us. We walk through into the parlor. Somehow our husbands fade away and I am conscious that it is just Vibeke leading me on. Our friendship is such a gift and I feel a sadness, wondering if Blixen had to leave such friendships behind in Africa when she returned to this home.

The walls are all painted, a darkness here, a lightness there; the house feels like it has been molded to sit beside the sea. The rooms are taller than they are wide, almost narrow—as is often the Scandinavian way—and the windows that stretch from the floor to the ceiling lead out to a veranda along the side of the house. One window is open and the long lace curtains that reach the floor wave and flutter but do not lift away, caressing the window as the breeze blows through them, waiting perhaps for someone's return. This room holds paintings. There is Farah Aden, Blixen's Somalian butler and beloved confidant. His portrait is hung high on the wall, staring down at us as if to give permission, or not, to our crossing another threshold and into the study. A room beside it is gently roped off, but we can enter the study (maybe because there is no one else there with us). These windows look out over the Oresund Strait and the water seems to shimmer back at us. It is a simple room where Blixen brought her memories. Here, hanging proudly on the walls, are the shields and spears of her people—maybe even of Kinanjui, the chief of the Kikuyu tribe, who lived on the farm. Did he—they—give these mementos to her? Did she take them, hungrily holding on to the farm, the freedom and the love that she found there for seventeen heart-filled years? I stand in this room for a long time before we retreat through the house, absorbing just a haze of understanding of the courage it took to live her life in Africa, and then, with heartache, returning home to Rungstedlund. Blixen brought only a few possessions from Africa: an old chair that was favored by her lover, Denys Finch-Hatton, and some glassware. Most of her belongings had been sold to a friend, helping to pay off the debts that were left in Africa.

Vibeke leads me outside and we walk through the forty-five acres that are now a bird sanctuary rather than the grounds around a house. It must have seemed huge and endless to Karen, growing up a child in this family home. I could see the magic through a child's eyes and then a child's memory merging into the lost imaginings for the returning woman. The forest becoming a wood, the river a stream. Blixen would have walked in this forest and in the winter light under the trees, so dark and Danish, cradling her memories of an African brighter light, sage brush desert, coffee trees, and love. I felt the sadness of leaving a beloved place and people, and maybe the remorse of failure.

Karen Blixen is laid to rest under the shade of a big beech tree that must have been there before she was born. There is an inscription on the simple slab over the grave, and carefully laid cobblestones fan out like a protective skirt against those of us who come to stare, though it is easy to imagine the woodland creatures taking their turns to join her in rest, lying on the cool stone.

Only later, when this visit was but a memory, I wondered: where did *Babette's Feast* come from? Was it the winter light on the water that brought out the loneliness of her life now? Did she turn from the memories of light and love in Africa to the cold damp winters of Denmark? These stories slipped into my consciousness quietly but they lingered, stored safely for comfort and courage.

The day ended and we said goodbye to Philip and Vibeke, returning to London for the Christmas break, our first ever away from our children and their families. The following year, 2013, was a year of constant travel together and apart. I dipped into the farm, grabbing the weeks and months to do what I could, yet knowing I was falling more and more behind in maintaining any semblance of active farming. What fruit I had hoped for Walter from the teaching seminar in Copenhagen was not yet ripe. There was the lure of another big film shooting in Vancouver, albeit with post-production in Marin County, to be followed by a documentary in London. The gears of Walter's life were not winding down, but ratcheting up.

* * *

In 2013, while Walter continued working in New York on *Particle Fever*, the quieter moments came. What was to have been a three-month project was becoming fifteen, but somehow the bicoastal commute still seemed reasonable to handle. We continued our practice of writing letters to each other every day we were apart. What began as physical letters in the '60s became faxes, before the introduction of email. Sitting down to write, each to the other, remains a daily focus and meditation during these times of separation. Now my time alone was producing a stillness that allowed for an unnamed longing to emerge and I began to record the daily life of the farm. I did not know then that 2014 would be the last full year spent at the farm.

Journal and essay scribblings became typed pages, with a few getting published in small local journals. Maybe the rest might become a family scrapbook of memories of what it was like growing up on the farm. But what was that like? Our jumbled family on a few acres of California coastal land unsuccessfully wrestled into a country home by an English Mother Hubbard and a filmmaker father whose stamina for film hours ofttimes outweighed that of his peers. When Robert Dalva's wife, Marcia, once commented to her husband about his long editing hours away from home, with his back literally to the wall, he replied, "Well, at least I'm not Walter."

Chapter 2

Winter 2014

Mushrooms and Mud

Finally, the soft Irish rain days, teasing us to turn on the windshield wipers, have given way to real rain. It started a few days ago. Leaving puddles, streams running and slick mud on the trails of Arroyo Hondo. The wind has brought the first of the eucalyptus and oak limbs down to the executioner's block. There will be more, but now that these old limbs have fallen and are cleared, the roads will be safer.

The tide is high and the lagoon flat and stoic as it takes a drumming from the rain. The duck field, now owned and worked by Star Route Farms and the Canadian geese, is flooded, and this is a good sign. There are not many of us who remember and miss the *clack-clack* of Fritz Meyer's winter dawn duck hunting.

Now, in early winter, after these first serious rains, Walter is home and we walk together along Arroyo Hondo Creek trail. Fresh fungi are bursting out of the underbrush, peeking through new green grasses and brown twigs. Different varieties seem happiest climbing huge, tall bay trees, themselves searching for the light and now decorated with the white blooms that almost look to be laughing. There are shades of brown, yellow, white, and, occasionally, red. The colors of autumn turning into winter. Mushrooms, like sorrow and grief, must rest deep down in the nourishing soil. Only later, when chilled and then soaked by nourishing rain, will they rise again in the winter light.

Driving a car around the lagoon and up north you can see the traces of foragers out hunting for the hidden porcini and chanterelle mushrooms of our woodlands. A truck parked here, a car parked sideways off the road there, but the hunters must be quick and, like pirates going to their hidden rock caves, slip in and out of the forests so as not to give away their secrets, and before the next incoming storm crushes the next flush of mushrooms emerging.

Then a real storm, the rain driving hard through the night, the wind blowing loose the fence line behind the greenhouse. We are all cold. Loose boards are blown free from our fences and the deer can hop over if they want to seek more shelter in the greenhouse. There are clusters of ladybugs, known as lovelinesses, in the bathroom and the study. They are huddled, safe from the drowning water outside.

Is it from being so dry or from becoming so arable that Gospel Flats are so deeply flooded this morning? The rain has not let up and is forecast to continue today. Water is pouring off the Mesa, cutting through the back hillside behind the fields, and dividing as it reaches our back garden and the mound. Some goes to the right, behind and around the Franklin farm, and the rest pours into the greenhouse and the back garden, the back field, and the barn. I dug a little trench by the barn, drawing the water away from there. Redirecting water is satisfying work. Soon after Warren and Marion Weber bought their first forty acres next door to us and trailered in a train caboose to make their home, moving water is how Warren and I first got to know each other. Many (many) years ago, we spent mornings bent over shovels, creating a pathway and moving silt and water as it rushed down the hillside from the property above and between us.

Today, the water is managed better. The homestead above created a back ditch and berm. Warren has tile drainage, and I added a plain ditch that slices through the farm from top to bottom. But still, the rains can overflow from that back boundary gully and berm, flooding through the fields to the front ditches. This morning, it has reached the back driveway and is backing up, creeping into the barn. While it keeps raining, the water will not leave until the little stream pathway I am creating is clear and flowing.

Winter Solstice

Gone from Mickey Murch's Gospel Flat Farm Stand are the pristine, tall, elegant leeks of the late summer and fall. Mickey's are priced at $1 to $2 a stem and are a bargain, at that. These leeks look to have been grown in a low spot and possibly got underwater and were flooded in the winter storms. Some of them are small; all are stubby with the long tops cut off. Rummaging in the bin, I pick out two fat ones at $1 each. They need a lot of washing when I get home as they are embedded with mud. All morning, the kitchen is full of the smell of home-made chicken stock with the leek tops. It is good.

Winter solstice afternoon, and Patricia Briceño is holding her lovely holiday art-and-craft fair on their barge at the far end of town, overlooking the lagoon. Patricia is a heart's art-work in herself, quietly and steadily drawing in women artists close around her, weaving a web of friendship that we all can share. Susan Martinelli is sitting at her table and has her knitting goods; pots of jam; and wool from her sheep, which is dark brown (because her husband Gurukar Martinelli forgot to give instructions to keep the fleeces separate); and a big basket of persimmons.

"Oh, you have persimmons."

"Yes, so many. Aren't they beautiful? Always in spring, summer, fall, and even winter."

"My tree gave me my second crop this year."

"How long before the first crop?"

"Seven years."

"Our tree too. I had to show Sarah Hammond when it first fruited. Her tree was the same."

"It takes seven years," Sarah had said before she left town.

It's true for all three of us and our trees.

"Who bought Sarah Hammond's place? Michael and Joshua bought Jo's place, Susie bought—"

And so it goes. The town is changing again, and we are becoming memories.

But the persimmon tree did give us her fruit. Maybe a dozen persimmons this year. Then she shed her leaves quickly, holding onto them only for Thanksgiving Day before letting them fall softly away to the ground.

Persimmon Pudding:

8-12 servings

- 3 pounds of very ripe Hachiya persimmons

- 1½ cups of milk

- 1¼ cups heavy cream

- 3 eggs

- 1 tablespoon honey

- 1¼ cups unbleached flour

- ¾ cup sugar

- 1 teaspoon ground cinnamon

- ¾ teaspoon baking soda

- ¾ teaspoon baking powder

- Pinch of salt

- 6 tablespoons unsalted butter, melted and slightly cooled

- 1 cup (about 6 ounces) of walnuts, toasted and chopped

1. Preheat oven to 325°.

2. Butter a 9-inch round cake pan and line with wax paper.

3. Cut out the core from each persimmon, cut them in half, and scoop out the flesh.

4. Puree the flesh and measure out 1½ cups to use.

5. Combine the persimmon pulp, milk, cream, eggs, and honey.

6. Lightly whisk until smooth.

7. In another bowl, sift together the flour, sugar, cinnamon, baking soda, baking powder, and salt.

8. Add the persimmon mixture to the flour mixture a little at a time, whisking until smooth.

9. Let the batter stand about 15 minutes to thicken.

10. Stir in the melted butter and walnuts.

11. Pour the batter into the prepared pan.

12. Bake in the center of the oven for 1-plus hours, until the pudding is completely set and pulls away from the side of the pan.

Serve the pudding warm, with lightly sweetened, cognac-flavored whipped cream.

Watercress

There has been no more rain, yet the grass is green and the roses are blooming! This morning, a hummingbird sat still on the arching rose branch of the Cécile Brünner fence. For a minute, at least.

"Look at the watercress. See it growing? There it is," my mother would always call out as we drove over a little stone bridge traveling through Hampshire. In the late 1950s, she would be driving, my father sitting beside her while I was perched in the back, taking in as long a view as if we were traveling by train. We would be going on our way somewhere deeper into the county or even on our way west to Dorset, Devon, or Cornwall. Passing through Arlseford always meant we were on an adventure, so I did look at the bright-green watercress as we passed over the bridge and the stream glistened in the sunlight, twinkling along with the fresh clear water. For some reason, I remember it always being sunny when we crossed the bridge. There was no end or beginning to the growing watercress. It seemed to jiggle along the side of the road through the village, bobbing on the moving water. Even then, I understood that moving water was a key element for the growing watercress.

Those were the days of mustard and cress sandwiches, watercress soup, and leafy green bits sticking out of our mouths on sunny summer afternoons. In England, watercress (*Nasturtium officianale*) is now barely in fashion, usually only for those times when one is making a point of being English. In the US, watercress can be found lying limp and faded yellow in plastic bags in the supermarkets. No wonder no one buys it. But with careful hunting it can now be found in the farmers markets again.

In Northern California, watercress is best scooped out of the streams, just after the first rains, and brought home for soup in winter and sandwiches in summer, harvested before the plant begins to flower for the best flavor. Then, when flowering begins, let it rest. Let the plants have their time to flower, bloom, and die until the next year.

When Pine Gulch Creek wakes up, the water skips over the stony gravel bed, turning rocks and pebbles, loosening fallen branches, twigs, and leaves, and pushing with an enthusiastic force along its course and eventually into the lagoon. But along the way, it sits in little alcoves and eddies, bubbling, still coursing its way down to the lagoon; it is here that watercress can grow.

Though it is still just January, we are already fearful of a drought. There looks to be no further rainfall this winter. Which means the wonderful flooding we had in December may not be enough to sustain the farm this year.

Blackberry Farm is on the flats, so we get the water that overflows from the Mesa and hillsides around us. Even with our mindful hedging and ditching, water flows and sometimes lingers in the orchard and fields beyond. It is in these ditches—the farm ditch we put through the fields, and then the roadside overflow—that the watercress grows. At first, I didn't recognize it. It was buried under the chopped-up sod and marsh grasses that invade the fields the moment nobody is looking. After forty years, I have given up that fight and will let them grow. Even Mickey doesn't bother with that corner of our field. But when the water is flowing through the ditches, the watercress is prolific and happy in its yearly spreading and exploring. If there was clay in the stream beds, the cress would taste even better.

When harvested as it is first emerging, it is at its sweetest and will sparkle in your salads, suffer bravely through sautéing, and smile smugly in a leek and watercress soup. As it ages, the stems become longer, searching out the sun and drawing water into itself; the leaves fade, just a little, in color. Watercress is tough yet delicate, like a seasoned character actor. At this age, it is resigned to soup which, as its name suggests, can be a watery affair unless thickened with potatoes. If you catch the seasons right, winter's end and spring's beginning, and spice it with the wild French sweet garlic that grows in abundance alongside the white narcissus, it becomes the nectar of renewal.

This recipe for sorrel soup is adapted from one given to me by my friend Creta Pullen. It was Creta who gave me my sorrel starts. I now have three plants and already cut and share starts from those plants.

Watercress or Sorrel Soup:

Serves 2 (with seconds) or 4 as a starter

- Use watercress or sorrel. Both produce lovely here-comes-spring soups.

- Harvest a big bunch / handful of watercress.

- And if you have it (what West Marin garden doesn't?), a spadeful of wild French garlic, or

- leeks, or any mild onion of your choice.

- Turmeric

- 4 bay leaves

- 1 big russet potato

- Leftover white wine

- 4 cups homemade chicken or vegetable stock

1. Wash and sort the harvests, and set in a jar with water until you are ready to use.

2. Sauté the wild garlic or a chopped onion or skinny leek in olive oil.

3. Add a teaspoon of turmeric and 4 bay leaves.

4. Stir to soften while dicing a russet potato.

5. Add the potato to the onions and stir some more.

6. Any white wine in the fridge? A glug or two can go in now.

7. After the wine is absorbed, add your homemade chicken or vegetable stock.

8. Let it all cook gently until the potato is tender.

9. Strip the watercress leaves from their stems and add to the pot.

10. While the soup cools, do something else (lay the table, boil an egg or two).

11. Fish out the bay leaves and put them in the compost

12. With whatever blender technique you use, blend the soup and watercress leaves together.

13. Return to the pot and adjust the seasoning. I add a little salt and pepper here.

14. Now, it is time to add your own favorites. This evening, we each had a just-turned boiled egg and a drizzle of leftover cream on the top of the soup

A small side salad, some warm French bread, maybe a little cheese and a glass of homebrew cider, and there is your supper.

Chapter 3

A Little History: Heading North

Walter graduated from Johns Hopkins University and spent one month as a Burns night guard. I left my job at White Plains Hospital. We married on Friday August 6, 1965, and walked back along Riverside Drive from the chapel at Riverside Church to Walter's parents' apartment, where our small gathering of family and friends celebrated with sandwiches, cake, and tea. Changing into our jeans, we packed up the BMW R50 bike and began motorcycling our honeymoon for six weeks, across the United States from east to west, and setting the kickstand carefully down in Los Angeles. Thanks to a full fellowship that paid both his tuition and $200 a month in living expenses, Walter entered the University of Southern California's film school, and I began nursing in the school's clinic and hospital, each of us finding our paths, side by side, as the strands of love that bound us were stretched taut and made tight.

A small group of friends found each other while lounging about in the grass courtyard of USC, and formed a nucleus that would grow and enter all the areas of our lives. At their very beginning, a seed was sown when their teacher, Gene Peterson, instructed them to "Get out now. There are no jobs for you in Hollywood." Film jobs in Los Angeles were few and far between. But many in that small group began finding and grabbing opportunities as they appeared. George Lucas found Francis Coppola when he was chosen for an internship at Warner Brothers. They bonded over their beards and soon set out across country, Francis to make *The Rain People* and George to document the making of the film. George had beaten out Walter for this Warner Brothers fellowship, but they had made a fraternal pact: Whoever got it would hold out a hand to the other. It quickly became clear to Francis—whose ideas are often immediate and precise—that if you can make a film on the road, you do not need to be in Hollywood; you can make one anywhere. The search began and the ended with a lightbulb moment after visiting John Korty in his studio in Stinson Beach. Francis returned to San Francisco and founded his independent film company. American Zoetrope was born in 1969. A small band of us—Francis and his wife Ellie, George and his wife Marcia, Walter and I headed north, making homes where we could.

We were kids, with a kid and no fear. At twenty-seven years old, we carried the confidence of ignorance, invincible as we faced a new adventure. There must have been a timeline but, as all things are in the film industry, it was short; weeks, not even months. Paying $16.99 each at the gate for a ticket on PSA, we boarded a plane from Los Angeles to San Fransisco. Picking up a Dollar-a-Day rental car, we drove over the Golden Gate Bridge and pulled into the Mill Valley Fireside Motel, Unit Two, by Highway 101. Ready to camp out for the weekend, we unfolded *The San Francisco Chronicle* and began our search.

We looked at dark, sunless apartments in the city and suburban-styled houses in Mill Valley, and climbed into the nighttime wet fog of the mountain over Muir Woods. By Sunday afternoon, having packed up and left the motel, we were ready to return to the city when Walter remembered his boss Cal Bernstein's suggestion. An independent filmmaker based in Los Angeles, Cal had recently returned from shooting a twenty-minute promotional film for United Airlines in San Francisco.

"Check out the houseboats in Sausalito."

We veered off the next exit ramp, doubled back under the freeway, and turned onto the gravel road at the Blue Bait Shop. The Gate Five Marina was ahead of us, where we were quickly lost in a maze of boats, homes, and dogs. Disheartened, we returned to the car. But before we went back to the highway, something pulled us to the right, along another slightly raised gravel road to a smaller group of boats on a single pier. A makeshift gate opened onto a flimsy narrow dock where boats and homemade homes, roped to cleats, rocked in harmony with the breeze and the tide. Halfway down the dock we came to a hand-painted *For Sale* sign outside a shack. During the last two years, we had been living off Walter's scholarship, spending all of my salary on cheap summer trips to New York and England, visiting our families. But not this summer. With the money we had saved there was enough: $5,000 for a down payment on a $7,000 houseboat at Gate 6½ in Sausalito.

The adventure unfolded fast as we shuttled back and forth between Los Angeles and San Francisco. In the previous two-plus years, I had begun to find my way around our small corner of Los Angeles. As a nurse and about-to-be new mother, I was afraid of losing those things I had put in place. Nurses chose their doctors with great care: My evening teammate, Anna-Lee James from Kentucky, great-granddaughter of Jesse, with flaming red hair and no fear, shepherded me to Dr. Harvey Chrystal, whom we watched from the nurses' station, noting how he treated his patients carefully and with courtesy, as well as sharing his extensive knowledge. He was an almost-as-young-as-us doctor, in harness with an older colleague whom we revered.

And then I was pregnant and feeling it, panicked at the thought of giving birth in America.

"Go and see Morgan Lord Morgan. Just to look at him will make you feel better," said another nurse friend, Delores. (MLM's name is not a typo.) And she was right. There were two Morgan brothers, David and Morgan, bright young men who started out by joining an obstetric and gynecological partnership known for being sympathetic to women who were exploring a new wave of natural childbirth practices. When I said I wanted to return to England to have my baby, Morgan replied, "It is your baby, you can have it wherever you choose." And with those words, I took courage and gained confidence and a sense of safety.

A few months later, Morgan's uncle, Gilbert Morgan, owner of the well-known Morgan Camera Shop in Los Angeles, became my patient. Though I wasn't expecting either of his nephews to visit, it was a surprise to look up from the nurses' station and to meet the warmest of smiles and a soft voice uttering a courteous introduction: "Hello, I wonder if I could see Mr. Morgan. I'm Dr. Kegel, a friend of the family." I'm not sure I managed a reply to his smile. Maybe he could already see I was pregnant. Though not yet in need of his world-famous exercises, it was hard not to stare in awe at this man whose work had benefited millions of women. At seventy-four years old, he was charming, trim and dapper, wearing striped trousers, a black jacket and, yes, a flower in his buttonhole.

Young Walter was born at the Good Samaritan Hospital in Los Angeles. Six weeks later, Dr. Morgan Lord Morgan slipped the speculum from my pelvis and rolled back his stool; I hadn't even had time to take my legs out of the stirrups before he said, "Right, you're good to go. Now speak to _____ and train as a Lamaze childbirth teacher." I did manage to take the classes and was prepared to teach, just as we were now about to leave LA.

Walter had been assembling the soundtrack for *The Rain People* in what was to have been the baby's bedroom in our little house on Cheremoya Avenue. The baby was moved into the tiny dining room, and we were back to eating in the kitchen. A few months later, we loaded up a rental truck with some furniture and the sound-editing equipment. Then it was on to Francis and Ellie's now almost-empty home to load up the rest of the post-production equipment that Francis had acquired. The U-Haul was full and I began the drive north out of Los Angeles. Walter quickly fell fast asleep on the long bench seat, his head in my lap, our son lying on the floor, as I drove to San Francisco. It must have been some kind of juggling act, with stops to feed father and son before arriving at Folsom Street, where we unloaded the equipment and Walter.

The next weekend, it was Walter's cousin, Tom Scott, who drove me and our son back north again, with the last of our small possessions, including a fuchsia from the Akron store, that made up our home. They were transferred to the houseboat and left, while we camped in the city to finish the mix of *The Rain People*. A pattern had begun.

When the film mix was finished, we eased ourselves onto our floating home and entered the houseboat community where we were accepted, making friends that have remained lifelong. The seeds of comfort found in this community were planted well in the soil of friendship, and I started to rebuild my life again.

As we settled into the houseboat, Walter began working with George, writing the screenplay for *THX-1138*. Now it was time to pick up the phone and knock on doctor's office doors, making tentative connections to a seriously suspicious medical fraternity and to begin teaching those childbirth lessons I had learned. Out of two-plus pages in the Yellow Pages, a handful took my telephone number, and probably used that piece of paper under their coffee mugs. But there were more patients asking to be engaged—prepared, even—for their childbirth experience. It wasn't long before pregnant mothers and the fathers came down the dock and rocked onto the boat. I could fit four couples at a time on the floor, and somehow, we did. City College in San Francisco was also looking for childbirth teachers, so I started a weekly class in a church close by Taraval Street in the city. Here, the church space was crammed with twenty couples, each with two pillows and a blanket, learning all they could, grasping and clasping their bodies to themselves. In each class, there was always one single mother with no partner, who was, even more than the rest of us, a stranger to San Francisco. These single young women became the women I partnered with as I taught, at times cradling them in my arms, willing them to relaxation, diffusing whatever courage I could into them for the journey ahead. I don't know how many got to see their babies after they were born or how many changed their minds and did not return to where they had come from but stayed in the Bay Area to begin a life with their child. I loved to teach, loved those families crowding into our little boat and the weekly adventures into the city. I was less lonely in the evenings.

Soon after we arrived, we claimed a tired 1964 White Ford Ranchero from an automotive dog pound in Mill Valley, brought her back to the Gate 6½ houseboat's unpaved parking lot, and let her rest. Moderately priced at four hundred dollars, the Ranchero was already past her menopausal prime. The three gears and reverse shift were on the steering wheel, with the choke-pull on the dashboard below. The little truck was perfect for the necessary motherly puttering in Marin County and occasional trips into San Francisco. Three mothers, Judy, Jill and I, and our toddlers, Cindy, Ted, and Walter, could all squeeze into the red-leather front (there was no back) bench seat. Pillowcases filled with laundry were tossed into the back for our weekly trip to the co-op grocery and laundromat in Corte Madera. Returning, we had three families' worth of groceries and the now relatively clean laundry, all stacked neatly into the truck bed. One mother took the children to her houseboat for sit-on-the-floor snacks, another brought the wheelbarrow of groceries and laundry back to our respective boats, and the third stayed by the truck to make sure nothing was stolen before it was all unloaded.

The little white truck was happy, cruising not too far in either direction up and down Highway 101. And then, in the fall of 1971, came the challenging question: Could the Ranchero make it down Highway 101 all the way to Los Angeles and back? It was discussed. Would it, could it, at not too fast a speed, but steadily, without overheating? I was firmly reminded that when the red engine light turned on, it meant something was happening and I should stop. But we were game, the little truck and me. My three-year-old companion, our son Walter, was strapped into a car seat beside me. Johann, our adopted half-wolf husky, the tricycle, and the driftwood-firewood gift for cousin Tom were crammed into the back. Walter had already left, and like Army camp followers of old, we were to follow. We drove for two days, arriving safely with not-yet-faded freeway memories of Hollywood, to stay with Tom while Walter worked on finishing The Godfather's sound effects and mixing post-production in Los Angeles. The Ranchero basked in the sunnier climate and softer grades of Southern California and was happy cruising back and forth between Los Angeles and the Santa Monica beaches. Weekly, we swung through the gates of the Paramount Studio lot for lunch or supper with the Godfather post-production crew. The little truck drew smiles of delight, and memories: "My uncle / grandfather had one of them." Returning up north, the little truck labored, even as we traveled slower still. We had no idea what changes would come for all of us with the release of *The Godfather*. It was a relief to be back home.

We were among a few houseboat families soon getting ready for our second child. Each of us sadly acknowledged we could not manage two children, dogs, laundry, and groceries on a wheelbarrow while living on our boats. As mothers, we were nervous, knowing we would have to leave the houseboat life, this small community we had made and come to love as our families grew. The men must have been worried also. For them, a bigger family brought more responsibility, and our husbands were all financially challenged in their chosen lives. But those ties of friendship remain as tight as any cleat hitch that moored our houseboats to the docks. To this day, we have remained close, making time for and with each other as our lives unfold.

We had looked as far away as northern Mendocino County, and sometimes still drive by a ninety-nine-acre holding on Route 20 that we walked over so many years ago. Most of the hillsides were covered with fallen logs, splayed across each other with storm-tossed, drunken abandon. Even in our youthful foolhardiness, we knew they would be too much for us to clear. Chuck and Judy did move to Mendocino, first to manage the Boys Club Camp, and then to a home in Fort Bragg and a rental machine shop. There, Chuck could share his expertise with foresters, ranchers, and other growers before retiring to his childhood love and becoming the tour guide and engineer on the Skunk Train. Meanwhile, Judy took up her role as childbirth teacher and labor coach, and remained vital to their hospital until her retirement. Ron and Jill slipped into Mill Valley, while they could just afford it, and raised Ted and Ami there. We got our break from Mrs. Phillips.

In the late '60s, few national or even regional California supermarket chains had reached Mill Valley. Among them were Lucky's and Cala, but not yet even a Safeway. There was the

Big G on Bridgeway in Sausalito, but that was more expensive. Shops were still shops, small and functional, each with its own specialty. Three hardware stores, maybe two bookstores, barbershops, and restaurants. There was nothing fancy, until along came the Phillips Coffee and Tea Shop, next door to the small Mexican café beside The Two A.M. Club. As a couple, the Phillipses had found a way to be and stay together through what must have been difficult years, as they acknowledged they both enjoyed the company and physicality of men. Mr. and Mrs. Phillips—we never did learn their first names—weekended in Bolinas and were saving up to retire to Hawaii.

The news of the Coffee and Tea Shop opening was shared gleefully. Ofttimes Jill, who is Canadian and understood the importance of a good pot of tea, and I would bike with our preschool sons seated in plastic carriers behind us, from the Gate 6½ houseboat dock community along the newly introduced bike paths to Mill Valley. The shop was small, with every high shelf and lower counter space crammed full with teas, coffees, teapots, cups and saucers, and candy. We had to hold onto our toddlers tightly, for those little hands were all too eager to reach out and pull a china teapot, wool tea cozy, or the glistening wrapped candy off the shelves. Big golden urns were stacked high above and behind the counters, as most of the tea was sold in bulk. Names like Assam, Ceylon, and Pekoe were found on the sacks in the back room. These teas were new in rural California, though commonly found in the hallowed caverns of Harrods Food Hall in Knightsbridge and Fortnum and Mason's in Piccadilly, London. Biking home, the anticipation of making a scalding pot of tea to sip on the sofa while watching the thick fog roll down the Waldo Grade in the late afternoon was a deep luxury. The coffee was no less exotic. Freshly roasted beans were dark to light brown. Imported, still by ships that had sailed from Colombia, Africa, and Arabia, the beans now lay bare under the glass of the front counter. We could choose from whole beans or ground coffee. The big scale and grinder on the back counter were all part of the magic of the store, and because we could order as little as a quarter of a pound at a time, we could afford it.

"There is a place in Bolinas. There has been a divorce in the family. I believe the old farmhouse and four acres are being split and sold off from the rest of the property." There had indeed been a divorce in a family, and now the bottom four acres and old farmhouse of the Peters ranch were up for sale. Later, we learned that when the widowed Mrs. Peters had sold the whole ranch, she had been promised a forever home, but maybe, lost in the old house without her husband or feeling the anger of divorce drift down from the hill above, had moved to safer, calmer surrounds in the community of Petaluma. Alicia, the last of us to stay on the boats, was a real estate broker in a realm still dominated by men and the only one of us who was not tied by husbands or children, and she checked it out. Alicia did this for us all, as we, her friends, moved away from her and the boats well before she was ready to leave the dock life. Indeterminately older than us, she was worldly wise in ways we only stumbled into. She set us all up, gently nudging us into our respective corners of the world as a friendly surrogate aunt would to stray young children. Alicia looked at the farm and talked with the broker, and very carefully kept us away from the seller. She took us to visit old friends of hers, Paul and Hilda Forman, who lived in town. We lay out on the bluff below their house as they chuckled that the ocean was claiming a foot a year in tithe for the view that unfolded before them. "If we were your age, we would buy it."

And so, in the summer of 1972, we did, not knowing at all what we were doing.

The farm was called Peters Dairy. When Manuel Antonio Goncalves received his US naturalization in 1920, he also took his new name of Manuel Soares Peters. His papers state his occupation as dairyman and he married Mary in Petaluma on September 30, 1930. When we first arrived, people told us how they still remembered getting their milk and eggs from the Dairy. It takes time for names and ownership to change. It doesn't just happen with a piece of paper changing hands. To this day, it takes replacing your own fenceposts, not remodeling the kitchen, to become an old-timer.

Later that year, while we were still living on the houseboat, my mother came for a visit. At the least, dubious, and more probably horrified as we turned off the freeway and onto the dirt road behind the bait shop, she managed to draw a breath and say, "Well, the main thing is as long as you are happy."

Three weeks later, she was thigh-high in the Richardson Bay, helping us move yet one more boat, Alicia's, onto its new flotation. Wearing my denim overalls, with a third-emptied brandy bottle sticking out of the hip pocket, she was loving every minute of her time with us in this warm and welcoming community. And I was pregnant again.

During that visit, we brought her to the farm, expecting the same kind of response to her first view of the boats. She was silent for a while, looking at this, poking at that, and then opened the decrepit barn door to the home of a wanderer. Who was that? Later I wondered if he was Ponderosa Pine or another who had taken his name from the woods. He emerged as if stepping out in front of a stage curtain and held two rainbow-colored candles, one in each hand.

"Peace unto you," he said as he gave my mother the candles.

"Thank you so very much," she replied as she took them from him. He retreated and shut the barn door. My mother kept the candles for the rest of her life.

"It will be hard work, but you will love it," had been her single comment. I took it as approval. Mothers know a lot more than we give them credit for.

It was a year later before we were finally able to move in. After a pregnancy spent mostly in bed, Beatrice was born prematurely. A month later, she tipped the doctor's baby scale at five pounds, and we felt fit enough to make the move. Our little family of four camped out downstairs in the house while we pondered what to do upstairs. Almost daily, I gathered up the little green frog that loved to cool down in the toilet bowl, placing it in the potted plant on the windowsill. One afternoon, Walter looked up from his place of refuge in the old bathtub and said, "I don't want to do a thing to this house." In that moment of stillness, I wondered what on Earth we had done. He had, after all, taken our houseboat shed and, with the help of the boat community and a box of Japanese hand tools, made it into a thing of beauty.

But I need not have worried, for the intrigue of building, the new canvas of the farm, and the obvious need of protection from the crushing wind inspired him to set to planing and framing a big greenhouse. Community habits of the houseboat life—watching out for each other's moorings in storms, joining together to help move each boat onto stronger flotations—slipped easily from boat to farm. By the following summer, as more friends from Los Angeles traveled north to visit, and then settle among those of us who were here, he was ready, and over a weekend gathered them with friends from work and new friends from town, to raise the framing and nail in place the siding of the greenhouse. We remain ever grateful.

Love at First Sight

While living on the houseboat dock at Gate 6½, Jill and I built a floating garden. There was a small, enclosed body of water where boats were not allowed to moor, as in old county plans there had been streets marked, waiting for the time this part of the bay would be filled in and the houseboats gone, making way for another kind of real estate. We scrounged old Styrofoam flotation and wedged hefty planks together. Another plank was the bridge across the enclosed body of water to the garden, which held two beds. We did remember to put life jackets on our boys as we built and then planted, watched in bemusement by other boat owners with more serious architecture on their minds. We found store-bought potting soil, but it was weak and porous, holding neither nutrients nor plants. Muck was needed.

Exploring on our bikes, we found our way to Tennessee Valley, and before the hidden cove and beach, there was a horse-boarding stable. We biked back and forth that valley road, bringing back cardboard boxes of manure, which were tossed and mixed into our little garden. It worked! We grew our first splendid zucchini—and confidence—that nurtured the buried seeds of our own gardening dreams. Maybe that little garden helped to pry us free from a water-bound existence. Biking hard uphill and fast down through that valley brought a glorious sense of freedom. And watching horses grazing in the wire-fenced pastures of the rough-and-tumble ranch unlocked my buried longing to ride. It had barely been ten years since I'd given my pony, Taffy, to another lost young teenage girl to care for when I left home for nursing school, and then to America.

There were ads in the local paper, *The Independent Journal,* and I began to read them.

* * *

The fuzzy bay head looked anxiously over the gate as I walked toward the walnut orchard in Novato. This family's teenage daughter was graduating from high school; her horses no longer held her heart and the orchard was to be sold for development. The mare had been given a quick hose-down and brush-up, leaving her short mane fluffy and wild, with her bright white star shining on her forehead. Her smallish ears were pricked forward, curious and hopeful of any interruption to this long, hot afternoon. The young black colt by her side was also bored and ready for his next adventures. The mare was thin, which accentuated her narrow chest. It was hard to see much quarter horse breeding in her, but she stood quietly as I ran my hands over her body, under her belly, and down her straight legs. She responded quickly and easily as I asked her to lift her hooves, one by one. I must have ridden her up and down the road, which was to become a boulevard before a year had passed. She moved easily and with no resistance to my guidance, and so a vet check was arranged. The following week, Bruce Daniels declared Babe sound in heart and limb, though her teeth—he shook his head—actually, her whole head was offset, as if the process of birth had squeezed her skull out of shape. Aged 'around eleven,' as with those teeth, it was hard to tell. But at $200, she was just affordable. Money changed hands and Babe was soon on her way to Tennessee Valley Stables and a larger pasture, where it didn't take her long to find her place in the herd.

And I in mine, among mostly young women and mothers who were only dimly aware of the threat to the tall, sloping wilderness, taking it all for granted. Spanish and Mexican ranchers had settled these hills in the seventeenth century before eventually giving way to Portuguese immigrant dairy farmers.

Roaming beef cattle gave way to dairy herds and hillside slopes were wired into pastures. We did not think about whose old ranches had been sold as families moved north. But in the 1950s and '60s, the Marincello Estate had been planned and begun as the gateway to development across the hills and high ridges, all the way to Sonoma County.

A loose but gathering band of far-thinking and reaching young activists, with names soon to belong to history—Huey Johnson, Doug Ferguson, Martin Griffin, Gary Giacomini, and others—held together and roped the developments to a halt, corralling Marincello and beyond into what was to become the Marin Headlands within the Golden Gate National Recreation Area.

Meanwhile, with my western saddle and grade mare, I was too intimidated to join in dressage classes that Angela Littlefield was beginning to teach at the Tennessee Valley stables. Instead, Babe and I took off through the already fading lettered gates of Marincello Estates and up the graded rocky trail that was never to become a road.

"Faster, Mummy, faster," was the urging from my now four-year-old copilot perched behind me in that western saddle. And Babe would break into an easy canter as if the urging was for her alone. The trail wound around and up the hills high above Marin City and we would soon be overlooking Waldo Grade as the afternoon fog rolled like thunderheads to cloak us in on the trail. The first time we climbed the trail, Babe slowed to a walk, then stopped to catch her breath. In the silence I sensed that we were being watched through the fog. Turning my head slowly, I saw, on a large rock not six feet away, my first red-tailed hawk. It was crouched and still, watching us and waiting for its moment. Even my copilot was quiet as we stood, while Babe continued panting softly, and we all listened to the wind. The fog was thick, moving in a pattern not yet of my understanding, but the hawk knew. A shuffle of her feet, a short fluttering of her wings, then, in the silence of the rolling fog, she took off, lifting for a moment before sailing down the lower ebbs of the wind gliding her way towards the valley below.

Those rides in the valley and up into the hills may have at first seemed an escape from the responsibilities of family, but they held the seeds to another responsibility as I was embraced by the wilderness on either side of the trails we rode. It was my forty days in the wilderness. Tennessee Valley was always, and is now, a noted raptor haven. The eagles, hawks, and all other birds of prey are now watched, banded, and counted. Back then, it was the birds that watched and marked us.

★ ★ ★

Barely begun, the rides in the Marin Headlands came to a sudden end. The hills called me, even as I slowed my pace, riding at a walk, begging the universe that it wasn't so. As I accepted my enforced bed rest for the remainder of my new pregnancy, it was time for Babe to move to the just-purchased farm in Bolinas. The months ahead seemed endless.

Babe hopped willingly into Gretchen Giacomini's horse trailer and I followed in our 1964 Ranchero. We drove in tandem along the freeway north before taking the winding road to the end of Sir Francis Drake Boulevard at Olema. There, Gretchen signaled a left turn at the three-way stop and we wound our way through the final eleven miles to the farm in Bolinas. Babe bounded out of the trailer and held her head high to look around.

A shrill neigh greeted us. Sukie Forman's quarter horse mare, Heather, trotted over, ready to meet her new companion. Or her minder; Heather was restless and apt to get out of her pasture if she was bored. Sukie was slowly transitioning from ponies to her womanhood, but John Balzan, a young cowboy, was just able to keep Sukie and her mare close to the barn. At sixteen, John was lean and handsome, and had almost grown into his Stetson hat. He was a good hand with fences, posts, and wire clippers. He could make a Portuguese gate, and patch up the wire and wood fences that were only just hanging in place. It had been some years since Mrs. Peters's sheep had grazed her pastures and the fences were falling, dying and dangerous, into the blackberry briars. Bringing in Babe to keep Heather company would help keep both mares settled, the pastures down, and the farm looking lived in. As John fixed the fencing and took on the care of the pasture, he came into his own, growing up and away from his family ranch up Horseshoe Hill, while Glen Campbell sang, "Mamas, don't let your babies grow up to be cowboys."

Sukie, John, and I shyly stood together, watching the mares as they got to know each other and settled into the pasture. Sukie was not sure about this friend of a friend of her parents, but was happy to have Heather safe in good pasture and, with John's help, was willing to take care of the two mares.

The horses were both blood bays, cow ponies of a certain age. They made a pretty pair in the rough pastures. Heather was solid, chunky with quarters that let her hold hard back on a roped steer. She was built for work and 4-H and a ranch life that was fading from reality in this corner of Marin County.

Even to an English eye, used to hill ponies, cobs, hunters, event horses, and thoroughbreds, I could tell Babe was what in dog's terms could be politely called a terrier mix. My pony, Taffy, had been the same. A Welsh Mountain, crossed with whatever had been in the barnyard at the time of her breeding, but she had the instincts of all good Fell Ponies, and the same was true of Babe. Yes, there was quarter horse in there but also a touch of Tennessee walking horse and maybe mustang. Her legs were straight, and as the spring grass was eaten—along with my first crop of lettuces—her coat shone and glistened with health. A grade mare, and fit for what purpose? A few years later, I learned what a real cow pony she was.

* * *

It was a month after Beatrice's premature birth that we managed the move from the houseboat community in Sausalito to the farm in June 1973, and our little family joined Babe. Slowly I gained my strength back. We cleaned out the old dairy shed next to the barn and found the Peters Dairy sign. In a drawer in the farm shed was a small notebook with just a few entries on faded pages.

On one side of the barn, stale hay flaked away in old calving stalls and the remembrance of Manuel Soares Peters's dairy. The other side, along with the broken-down henhouse, had recently sheltered strangers.

I spent a lot of time in the kitchen, rocking a fretful baby while gazing out of the windows and watching children after school, riding their ponies fast alongside the road past the farm, over the hill and onto the beach.

After her dawn feedings, I could at times carefully lay Beatrice in our bed beside her father, letting her breath fall into a rhythm with his as she brought him the warmth I was taking away, and I could leave. By the time I was downstairs, the sky would be lightening and the morning air rising with seaside promise.

Under the old weeping willow tree, I gave Babe a quick brush, cleaned her hooves, and slipped on the bridle. We walked quietly down the driveway, not wanting hurried hoofbeats to wake anyone in the house. Babe was slight and her chest narrow, though deep. She stood only fifteen-point-two hands high, so my long legs fell below her belly, but she carried my weight well. Onto the grass verge beside the road into town, we swung into an easy trot—we didn't have much time—and climbed up Phinney's Hill. A bound, and we were in the eucalyptus grove heading down the other side and into the still-sleeping town. Maybe someone, hearing hoofbeats, would stir and wake from within a parked VW bus, or a sleeping dog might raise an eyebrow while it lay on the road. Young fishermen beginning their serious love affairs with the sea, a Knowles or Churchman, would loosen the ropes that moored their boats before heading out into the channel. The tide's ebb and flow changed each year, and in these years a medium low tide meant that both the channel and the beach were within reach. Slipping down the ramp on Wharf Road, we were on the sand by the channel. Babe pulled toward the water. She would paw, pound, and splash the waves over us both. By now, the sun would be over the trees, and more dogs, with and without their people, ran with their heads down, scavenging death on the beach. Depending on the beach sand's breadth, we could move from a trot to a barely contained canter, in the water, out of it, in and out, playing. It would be a brief moment, twenty to thirty minutes at the most, before turning up the Brighton ramp and heading through the other side of town, back home. Babe into her pasture and I into the kitchen. There would be the stove to light and coffee to prepare for a new day.

Chapter 4

"Welcome. What are you all havin'?"

If we had been inland, away from the ocean, things could have been different. Some rural communities have a Gun Club, others a Rod and Boat Club. And we are grateful that ours is the latter. There was a tough mellowness to this group, composed mainly of men. The early members of the Bolinas Rod and Boat Club, who weathered the storms of the 1971 San Francisco Bolinas oil spill, had also seen their real estate dreams of selling off a little bit of land here and there drift away as the tide brought in the oil and a new wave of immigrants from the cities. They soon found themselves living and working alongside these eager young families, whose passions and commitments were often in direct opposition to their own beliefs. A few were crushed, but others shrugged us off as the flotsam and jetsam that washed in with a high tide. That generation had seen too much, remembered too many losses, to let us get them down. They had age and experience, they were shrewd, and they could pretty much spot who we were before we knew ourselves. The Bolinas Rod and Boat Club was run in the late 1960s by Ed Letter. Ed and his pals—the Peppers, Smiths, Middletons, and O'Conners—were our forerunners, the old-timers of today. Building this, tinkering and fixing that, was the currency they dealt in while striving to make a living.

But the Rod and Boat Club had taken out a mortgage to buy the dock, the mud, the air where the houseboat clubhouse they had purchased was situated. These men disliked owing anything to anyone. Something had to be done, but what? In meetings among themselves, they asked what was missing from this town, and answered: a good Sunday breakfast.

As far as we could tell, when we first ventured through the door of the Rod and Boat Club and joined the line at the counter, the Pancake Breakfast was Ed Letter's show. After retirement from the United States Postal Service in San Francisco, Ed lived on the lagoon with his wife, Lillian. There was a small house-boat on the water and a small boathouse beside it. They really were about the same size, and it was hard to tell in which Ed spent more time. There were young fishermen coming up and a boat builder or two who slipped into Ed's cove for gear and guidance, and the secrets safely found in that man-cave. Ed was a boat builder, building his own and, on occasion, boats for others. Within those deeper tidal waters, boats could be hauled out of the lagoon at Ed's, winched up clear of the ground to be cleaned, repaired, and repainted. Hours, days, and weeks would go by for men to be men. And here, young boys such as our son and his pals, would take the thrilling adventure to bicycle from school to Ed Letter's boat shop on the lagoon. There, Ed would take the time for careful consideration of the merits of this fish-ing weight or that, which hooks did they need for the different rods, and the dreams of these young fishermen. All could be discussed and purchased without the interference of a mother. Ed cared for the men, the boys, and the water he loved.

Ed and Lillian have long since moved onto other celestial waters, but the house and boathouse remain on the lagoon, sequestered by the Golden Gate National Recreation Area. Lichen beards grow long on the California oak, brushing the red budding camellia shrub and hanging down over the drive-way. There is a squidgy feel to the ground, as if it is deciding whether to join the lagoon mud or linger awhile by the roadside.

No one could make pancakes to Ed's standard and without his direct supervision. So every two weeks, on Sunday mornings from eight to noon, Ed hovered over the volunteers in the Rod and Boat Club kitchen while they served up an all-American breakfast: orange juice, pancakes, eggs (how do you like 'em?), bacon, syrup, butter, and Folger's finest coffee and cream. No milk was skimmed, and no eggs, bacon, or butter were organic. We flocked to it. Young mothers were grateful to sit down and be served. Fathers were grateful for the extra cup of coffee and another hour or more of postponing Sunday's chores. It gave us a place to break bread together. Warring educators, parents, and old-timers poured each other coffee with an old-fashioned American courtesy. Families, friends, and, occasionally, visitors to town sat together.

Walter was allowed to join the Rod and Boat Club, but who let him and when is past memory. Possibly because we had arrived with a fourteen-foot rowing boat with a small outboard motor we had brought from the houseboat. He had looked promising, though the boat was stolen within a month of it being put in the water at the dock.

Slowly we came to know a few of the members, the ones who let us know them with a nod here and a howdy there. Maybe it helped that John O'Conner saw me riding as casually as the girls with their ponies. These men understood the importance of nurturing the next generation of farmers and fishermen and, though Walter was one of those artist fellows, he seemed to be making a living at it, and while not too available or handy by their standards, he would, on special occasions, such as Mother's or Father's Day, bring his Cara espresso coffee maker to Pancake Breakfast. A sign on the edge of the counter announced that, for one dollar, a cappuccino with frothed milk would be served in brown Italian cups. One dollar for a coffee. Whoever heard of such a thing?

It was on one of those Sundays, when Carol and Dexter Hake were walking by, that maybe they said to each other, "Why not?" before wandering in. Sitting in the sunshine outside on the deck, we shared a table.

"What is it like to raise a family here?" Carol asked. What did I reply, not knowing she was thinking of her young pregnant daughter, Sarah Hake, recently married to Don Murch? We had never met another Murch who was not family. I do not remember the words, only the warm, relaxing sunshine. Maybe something like... because even more then than now, I did not always taste my words before I spat them out. Having found my place working in Point Reyes as a community nurse-midwife, I could reply, "It's fine, great. I know most of the drug dealers and they know to leave my children alone." I doubt I spoke as I should have, more sensibly, about the small school and how as parents we really could have a say in our children's education.

Eventually, we gathered children from the sand of changing tides and made our way home to the farm. Carol and Dexter Hake took a stroll on the beach before going back into town and stopping at Louise Pepper's real estate office, where Louise had listed her husband's family ranch for sale.

The transition was gentle, the handoff of one retiring farmer to one starting out. There were old trees to discover and nurture. In 1972, when we arrived at The Old Dairy, Mrs. Peters's incredible green thumb was still visible, and to this day, the pear tree and her roses continue to flourish. The Hakes and their young Murches down the road at number 140 must have found similar treasures to welcome them.

As Don and Sarah moved in, they were supported by Sarah's parents. Carol settled in to paint, recording the changes of yet another farm and moment in history. Don began to work the river bottom land that had grown richer with each year it lay fallow. As the young energetic family took on the harness of work, the house shook off the dust of old years and sighed a deep, hopeful sigh.

Both families of Murches, staggered as we are in age like cousins often are, have gained encouragement, one from another. We are loosely joined, though no blood relation at all. Only visible in look: the dark Mediterranean eyes of Walter and Don speaking of Spain and Cornwall, and maybe just a hint of English milkmaids who have farmed at either end of Gospel Flats.

It was an easy handoff, like a nursing shift change of two RNs. As Helen Swallow packed up her home and left her office at the Point Reyes Medical Clinic for the East Coast and Cornell University to become a certified midwife, we moved into town and I stepped into the roster of nurse-midwives. In the early 1970s, Michael Whitt had answered a *Doctor Wanted* ad in the *Point Reyes Light* newspaper. Wes Sokolosky joined him a year or so later. Ed Kosinski cruised in on his BMW bike, and soon there were more BMW motor bikes parked at the doctor's office than at our farm. By the mid-1970s, there were three doctors and four nurses on weekly rotations, one nurse in the office, one on call, one off-duty, the other off for months with their own pregnancy and new baby or to catch the doubling up of births on bright, moonlit nights that so often happened. Unpacking our pots and dishes to reclaim a weary country kitchen, I carefully saved the boxes and newspaper, taking them to Helen's house on the mesa so she could pack, ready for her next migration.

By the time we settled into the farm, the Ford Ranchero was truly feeling her age and very grateful that the road to Point Reyes was relatively flat. From time to time, she would have us raise her skirt to find "where it hurt" under the hood. For a while we tightened this, rewired that, and poured oil into troubled cavities, but the knocking transmission was the death knell.

The Ranchero's demise was not made any easier by the addition of a shiny new Saab sedan car that arrived in gratitude from *American Graffiti*. With the success of *American Graffiti*, even more than *The Godfather*, the realization that it could be possible to make a living as a freelance filmmaker outside of Los Angeles began to really take hold. This was never going to be an easy path, but it was a possible one. The Saab was a commitment in that direction. It was a real European car that was happy to cruise over the hill to the city and back again almost every day. At first, the Saab was a little put out at being assigned to a farm with a dirt driveway, but soon settled to its work and enjoyed those trips farther afield, stretching out on the freeways with memories of fast European highways. But if the Saab was taking on the city run, there needed to be another cheap and cheerful motor which I could use for the daytime school and dentist trips, along with my nighttime midwifery calls.

The orange Chevy Vega wagon showed his breeding as he slouched like a lowrider, nosing up the driveway onto the farm. The Chevy Vega of 1974 was to become known as one of the worst cars that General Motors ever produced but, like many others, we had been tempted by the cheap price and the wagon hatchback. The Vega was all bravado and cool, but could easily be pushed off the road by any old truck that felt insulted by its very presence. For such a small car, it was surprisingly expandable, and with the windows open could take up to eight young soccer players. Trips to the dentists and supermarkets didn't faze the little Chevy, and the overflow of accompanying hamburgers, French fries, and ketchup blended effortlessly into the plaid upholstery. As for the nighttime midwifery runs, it easily cruised along the rural roads of Marin and Sonoma counties, reaching as far as Petaluma, Two Rock, Tomales, Nick's Cove, and Dillon Beach. The Vega wagon model had a nifty hatchback that could carry a full midwifery bag and any necessary blankets. The front seats fell back and the car was comfortable to sleep in as I pulled to the side of the road when exhaustion forbade me to drive all the way home. There were magical journeys; ofttimes racing to a family at the beginning of an evening labor, and then slowly driving home at dawn after a successful delivery. Leaving a young family to the wonder of birth and new beginnings, softly twisting through the forests of Point Reyes National Seashore, no rush now, my work done for the moment, there was time to pause and wonder at the beauty of an elk herd grazing close by, unfazed as they too protected their young.

The Vega was so brightly orange that, parked on the mesa or around town, it was easily recognizable. Between carpooling kids and delivering babies, the little car nudged me into my place in West Marin. But the unpaved roads of the Bolinas Mesa caught that Chevy up in every season. In 1976, the car was on its third oil pan by the time we had to leave for England, where Walter was to edit *Julia* for Fred Zinnemann. The Vega was moved on to a kinder, gentler home, but it never really recovered and continued to leak oil until its death in some bequeathed charity graveyard for automobiles.

Finding Mrs. Peters's Garden

In 1972, the front yard helped to give the dairy its new name: Blackberry Farm. It was covered in blackberry vines sliding under and climbing over the clumps of couch grass that tenaciously twisted their roots into the soil. It does not take long for couch grass (Elymus repens) and roaming blackberries to invade and capture low-lying fields that are sitting on an old riverbed. But under the overgrown wilderness, old gardens hold stories. Arline Bernstein writes in *Growing Season: A Healing Journey into the Heart of Nature* that uncovering them can reveal the secrets of the past and inspire dreams for the future and that, within a neglected garden, there are always enough treasures for soup.

Barely visible were the fallen fence posts holding crushed sheep wire across the width of the yard. Was it a yard? Was it a garden or was it a pasture? As we slowly pulled the wire out, took a mattock to the clumps of couch grass, and let the sturdy blackberry vines draw blood, it looked to have been all three in the forty-five years that it was tended by Manuel and Mary Peters. And when the Peterses took over from the Smiths, Mary Peters must also have discovered the treasures left by them. She would have brought them forward while adding her own dreams. People who remembered the Peterses always smiled when they spoke of the sheep grazing and the daffodils blooming in the spring through that front pasture. The sheep were long gone, but the daffodils remained and fought back, pushing past the couch grass and peeking up through the blackberry vines.

Now it was my turn. We did make progress cutting through the vines and lifting clumps of couch until spring on the farm was heralded by the small, single-trumpeted, pale-yellow narcissus minor daffodils. I only had a vague idea of what I was searching for or hoped to find when Walter brought me John Seymour's book, *The Guide to Self-Sufficiency*. Now I had my bible, guide, and purpose. Published in 1975, it spoke to many young families, would-be farmers searching for a path back to the land and into self-reliance.

Alongside many of the farmhouses of West Marin, you can still see the remains of the cypress trees that were planted to protect the farms. The Swiss and Portuguese farmers chose varieties that were tall and tough. Their job was to give partial shade to cattle in the pastures and, often as importantly, to protect the farmhouse and out-buildings from the high winds that bent all trees in their paths as they swept in from the sea, across mesas and plains, and dipped into the valleys below. But some trees did not last as long as the houses they were planted to protect.

The Smiths had planted two rows of cypress around the buildings, probably soon after they first built the farmhouses around 1880. There was one row that separated the two houses and another behind the tall farmhouse. The wind coming down off the hill from the mesa remains brutal, and this row of tight trees gave some protection to anyone who ventured outside. The Tacherra Ranch still has some of its trees; immensely tall and ancient, they are holding, somehow sheltered from the worst of the winds. Cypress roots are relatively shallow, while the trees can often reach eighty-plus feet in height. Depending on the winds and weather, it can be just thirty years before the cypress could begin to creak and sway. You can be startled awake in a night storm. A sound—is it a thunderclap, or is it a big and, you think, solid limb being torn from the trunk of the tree? Ripping one branch or two, the wind will find a pathway into and around the trees and carry on. And there is another death that comes from below, if mattress vine, Muehlenbeckia, has knotted into the base of the trees. The vines grow quickly, weaving in on themselves and climbing upward, circling the trunk and limbs of the cypress trees. This was the fate of the trees that had been planted at the back of the farm. Luckily, the vine had held the trees in place, strangling the trunks so that they sunk into the ground where they were rooted. They were matted thick with the vine, and the wind did not have the strength to blow through the trees onto the house. Mrs. Peters had been right to leave it all in place. Even the deer passing through the fields rarely ventured inside this enclosure.

The cypress trees were choked, broken, and buried by the vine. Even knowing that they still served a purpose in protecting the house from the wind, I only saw a hugely expensive farm chore that would have to wait—a long time. On the other hand, Walter saw a project and, with films and finances still as precarious as ever, and not quite ready to put his saw away in the shed, he set to, and a tree-fort was built where childhood secrets could be shared and left buried in the crevices of tree and vine. There was enough to explore and make tentative beginnings again.

Between the vine-covered cypress and the house was the septic tank—feeding, in its own way, the two remaining apple trees and other things yet to be discovered. The old henhouse—a wire pen in drooping tatters and bereft of chickens, but that had housed a Harvard graduate, by the look of the books left behind—remained. And there was the well. Covered with a rusted sheet of metal that wobbled at the slightest hint of a breeze, it needed serious attention if we were not to lose a child or two into its cavernous hole. Walter set to work on that also, and for a few years, the old windmill came back to life, pumping water to the tank on the hill behind us and back down to the house. It was clear that the placement of the water tank was set at a height so that a toilet could be flushed upstairs. An ivy hedge had grown over a small white picket fence that ran along the driveway side of the house. Somehow it had been propped up, and it sheltered the small path to the back door. Ripped away when we jacked the house up to replace the redwood foundations with concrete, the ivy and pale-pink tiny-blossomed fuchsias gave themselves an annoyed shakedown and continued to grow. Between the overgrown front yard, the ivy fence and the cypress-enclosed back garden, it felt as if, as they got older, the Peters had closed in on themselves. Maybe Mary even more so, after Manuel died. The farm was sold soon after, and Mary Peters moved to Petaluma, where she grew another kind of garden. Now it was my time to explore.

The two apple trees were a welcoming treat. I recognized the Cox parenting right away by the fruit's mottled color, crisp texture, remembered taste and aroma. But the trees were old and grown on a medium rootstock which, though popular, never had the strength of the standard trees. The apples stayed on the trees until late in the autumn, and were crisp and flavorful every day.

And there were roses to be discovered, buried in the overgrown grasses and weeds. A tall shrub rose with tight pink blossoms and a delicate fragrance that belies its toughness remained where Mrs. Peters planted her. What was it? Years later, I was able to produce two more from the original and they are as tough as their mother. The leaves get very little rust or insect damage, and they bloom at least twice a year. The storms don't damage them, the droughts don't kill them, and even crowding the roots with too many daffodil bulbs doesn't seem to faze them. The blossoms tempt me to bring the blooms into the house, where they last just a day. I like to think of Mary on a winter's evening, sitting by the stove, enjoying the early plant catalogues that began to arrive in the mail after the Second World War. And I like to think she had a post-war approving eye for English stock. She knew her soil and her climate, for the Laxton Fortune apples and this rose stayed strong on the farm. But there was another rose buried in the long grasses that I almost missed. At first, I had hardly glanced at the solitary stem, but in the first year, two small, bright red buds appeared. Nothing very impressive to look at, but the fragrance was strong and bold for such a little plant. What was it? I took a flower stalk down to Michael Bernsohn at the Las Baulinas Nursery, who easily identified it as the American Beauty rose. Now I had a rose with a name, and it needed to be saved and nurtured—but where? I moved her about, finding this spot and that. She survived my digging her up and replanting her here and there. She survived many deer onslaughts and kept coming back. Over forty years later, she is still safe in a fenced rose bed, though pouting with not enough sun. The American Beauty is tough and there is nothing subtle about her. Like much that is American and beautiful, the rose is an immigrant; French in origin, her first name being Madame Ferdinand Jamin. George Valentine Nash from the New York Botanical Gardens traveled, as botanists do, and it is said that he brought the American Beauty back from London's Kew Gardens in 1875, and tweaked her a bit, as Americans do. Improved, bigger, stronger, she became the rose placed in dining cars on long train rides across the country, and eventually found her place in those new catalogues. The American Beauty is the grandmother of the single-stemmed rose offered for sale on hot nights in the city for your sweetheart. Her picture could have shone out at Mary as a bright spot of color and hope in the cold winter evenings as she looked through the catalogue that had arrived in the mail.

Now our daughter-in-law Sirima goes through the farm garden with the same eye. She knows of Mrs. Peters's roses, the Louise Bonne pear tree, Aggie's apples and rhubarb. As she plants her dreams, maybe she will find the old China rose from whence all roses come.

Doctors Jesse and John

If I close my eyes to a half squint, Jesse and John come back into focus—sometimes arriving in an old truck that might have been red at one point, at other times on bicycles. Jesse Schwartz, tall, thin, wearing a red waistcoat and a black beret; and John Kozack, fit, shorter, sporting a gray shirt and yellow bowtie. Can that be right? But from this distance, it seems close. In the late 1970s, they had set out on a hunt for the heritage apple trees still to be found on the old farms that were changing hands. They already had a collection of trees that were clustered in overflowing pots and bursting out of a home in Berkeley. But now Jesse and John had the use of three acres tucked away in Paradise Valley in which to plant an apple orchard nursery, and in 1979 they founded the Living Tree Community. They searched out trees on ranches around town and the lagoon, and then traveled further north, east, and south in California and into other states across America. They talked to ranchers and acquired scion and brought it back with them, laying the bundles of labeled twigs out on their potting bench, ready for the root stock they found in Oregon. Then they began to graft scion, propagating their new old trees. Their little three-acre orchard was organically fed and nurtured with homemade compost, seaweed and water drawn from the creek that flowed through the valley. The trees they planted thrived.

We were a natural stop on their quest, and Jesse and John drove into the yard one day as people tended to do then. They had heard about our two old trees and asked to see them. They appeared like doctors and, like a good nurse, I showed them the trees, which immediately became patients. There was some serious standing about, followed by discussion.

"How are they doing?"

"Not very well," was my answer. This was followed by more looking at the bark, the branches, and maybe even some scruffy fruit. They came up with the name of the apple, Laxton Fortune, and got, in their fashion, excited. The Laxton Fortune, if this it proved to be—and it did—was a great find, a cross between the English Cox and the American Wealthy apples. It became popular in 1948 on both sides of the Atlantic. The apples were small by any standard, but sweet. Orange with a green blush, if I remember correctly. The Brogdale Orchard catalogue in England describes it. *"A Cox cross-raised by the Laxton Brothers in 1904, this shares the fine flavor of its illustrious parent. The medium-sized yellow-flushed red fruit are best left on the tree as long as possible to allow the sweet rich aromatic flavor to develop fully. Resistant to frost and a good cropper."*

Well, that seemed about right. It was defiantly sweet in flavor, and I credit Mary Peters good taste in choosing this apple. But now, the trees were failing. The old windbreak cypress hedge was falling down, and the mattress vine had taken serious hold of the cypress, snaking between crushed limbs and crowding out the sunlight. Maybe there was not enough air circulating around the little apple trees; maybe the medium height rootstock was failing; maybe they had not been fed, pruned, or loved for too long. Maybe all of the above. But for whatever reason, the trees were fading away and I was happy to have Jesse and John pay a house call.

It was decided that they would come back midwinter and take scion to graft. And this they did. Two years later, they returned with a couple of trees for us to plant. And the trees did well—for a while.

Jesse and John also did well, for a while. They seemed to float in and out of town, spending most of their time with their apple trees in Paradise Valley. They commuted from Jesse's home in Berkeley back and forth, but unless you were close to them, and their apples, it could be hard to know them. Jesse and John continued gathering scion, propagating and selling their two-year-old trees. Before too many years had passed, they had planted at least four rows of old apple-tree varieties, labeling and mapping them. It must have been grand to see, for they were careful and passionate men. They rediscovered and rescued many old varieties. Our Laxton Fortune was one, Newtown Pippins from old ranches by the lagoon, big green apples from Martinelli's, Thomas Jefferson's Spitzenburg (how did they get that?), and Hudson Golden Gem, a spectacular oval apple that smelled of pineapples. In the 1980s, they could boast they were the only nursery to grow the Ukrainian Reinette Simirenko apple, made famous for going into space with the Russian cosmonauts. Pink Pearl, Hauer Pippin, and Skinner Seedling were among their popular varieties, but the biggest rediscovery was the variety known as the Cinnamon Spice apple. Finding and propagating the old apple trees was hard graft, and even with their two-year-old saplings selling well, this was clearly not a moneymaking business.

Times were changing and Jesse found himself swimming against the tide of commerce with his heirloom apple trees. The heart was there, but his pockets were empty. Until one day, his curiosity and attention turned to almonds. When Jesse found almonds, he made almond butter. Soon, Living Tree Community Foods was born, and Jesse folded and gently put aside his fruit-grafting knife.

As he had drifted in, so he drifted out of town, leaving John and three acres of heirloom apples to the fog and the sun and the loneliness of Paradise Valley. There was a tattered map handed on from one farmer to another, each of whom was too busy with their own farms to pay attention to someone else's abandoned project. As Jesse had shown, there was no real money to be made in apple-tree propagation, or apples. Even the farmers further north, in Sonoma and beyond, were struggling, slowly uprooting apple orchards, turning the sod, adding a different fertilizer before layering their acres with grapevines. There was plenty of money in wine and almonds, but very little in apple juice.

It was a gentle fade, maybe more intense for the farmers driving past the neglected trees standing beside the dirt road that leads in and out of the valley. They were busy making as good a living as they could, growing organic vegetables and founding the Marin Organic organization. Jesse's and John's apple trees were planted close together and, over time, as they competed for water and nutrients, they began to weaken. Maybe it was Dennis Dierks who one day offered some trees to Don Murch at Gospel Flat Farms across the road, which lies halfway between Paradise Valley and Blackberry Farm. Don, now a farmer with a backhoe, came in and uprooted and retrieved several of the trees, replanting them at Gospel Flat Farms across the road. But it didn't take long before Don also realized he had too many trees crowding together, and gifted some to us. The trees left at Gospel Flat Farms breathed a sigh of relief and stretched their roots deeper into the soil. They had water and air and were protected by the farmhouse from the strongest of winds and the sharpest of heat. They were (as trees are) relieved to see their weaker brothers and sisters leave for another farm up the road. But the trees that came to us had been moved three times and, like military children during a late adolescence, became uncertain, surly, and cautious, unsure of themselves, wondering if it would be safe to really put down roots.

I had dreamed of an apple orchard, and these gifts from Don, added to my two Laxton Fortune trees, were my start. While we had made a new beginning to the farm in the '70s, now, as the years went by, it was changing again. The children were grown and on their life journeys, several horses were buried in the fields, and there was an uncertain shift on the farm. Maybe I could plant an apple orchard. I just had time, twenty years and counting, to begin and see the fruits of that harvest. Next there came deer fencing and a gate, and the small lopsided wire cages around the brave trees could come away. There was still no steady supply of water. Somehow that continued to escape me. But over the years, as more trees joined this rag-tag field, becoming an orchard, what did emerge were the apple varieties that truly thrive in our own microclimate.

★ ★ ★

When we drove into town in 1972, Ram and Marissa Fishman drove out, heading further north, and found Garberville. Young families were on the move. We were still in a time of all possibilities. Secluded and hardworking, Ram and Marissa set about creating Greenmantle Nursery, where they specialized in roses and apples. Did they stumble on Albert Etter's thirty-two-acre orchard at an elevation of 1,500 feet and begin to bring it back to life? Or was the goal always to search out apples and roses? Maybe it was the enticement of history in horticulture that set Ram and Marissa alight, to steadfastly learn and uncover the history of Etter and his trees. Albert Etter lived from 1872 to 1950. Seventy-eight was a long life for a hardworking farmer. One can suppose the orchard and land might have lain fallow or uncared for until Ram arrived. No picture of Ram and his wife exists on their website, and there is no email address with which to contact them. Ram and his Marissa have taken to the hills and buried themselves in a hidden spot of paradise. I was slow to find them. Hunting about for old apples, I stumbled across Ram's Greenmantle catalog, then dedicated *To all the Old-Timers, Long may they thrive.* Now it is us, we and the Rams of the world, who are the old-timers. And for me, there is a longing to put right what I have neglected for so long. My footsteps among the apple trees are still too few. Though lower in elevation, the climate Ram describes in Garberville on his website is much like it used to be here. So it is no surprise that the trees from Greenmantle have done better than those old beloveds moved from their first home in Paradise Valley. We are grateful for the Hauer Pippin, whose limbs bow low with dark-red apples of firm flesh and crispy texture, and that if harvested before the birds reach the fruit, will last through Christmas. Golden Russets for autumn eating; Wickson and Winesap, happy crabapples that just love to be crushed for cider; and the Waltana apple, which, had I been more mindful, could have survived and been a special treat for us all.

Being an apple man or woman is not a path to riches, and barely one to self-sufficiency. But love of the trees, the husbandry, and the fruit is as rich and aromatic as the love of any beloved, and, to me, quite different from the admiration of the exotic pear. Is the apple more commonplace, more workmanlike? Why do we gravitate to certain fruit—some that excite us in their difference, while others comfort us in their homely steadfastness? Sometimes I dream of days and evenings spent walking the farm orchard. In my dream I am my age now, with the patience and time of age, but with the energy of twenty years ago, tending each young and old tree more carefully, time making me a better guardian so they may live and bear fruit for another generation to come.

Jess Comes for Coffee

Jess Tacherra would have seen our family at the biweekly Pancake Breakfasts, where he was to be found working at the back of the kitchen. Though never like Sherman Smith—ready to pen a face on a child's knuckles as they clutched onto the bar rail—Jess moved slowly, carefully carrying a full plate of pancakes from the big hissing gas range to the counter. There would only be nodding acknowledgment across the counter that our eggs were ready to my "thank you," until the day he drove his old green Chevy truck up our driveway and came to a halt before the barn.

The farmhouse still looked weary and beaten-about after the previous few years, but now there were horses grazing in the pastures and children running noisily around in the yard. With a little help, old wire was being removed, and fence posts were straightened and even replaced. The mattress vine that had covered and continued killing the last of the windbreak cypress trees behind the farmhouse held the fort and treehouse Walter had built, with a little on-the-ground direction from his pal, the screenwriter Gill Dennis. The old chicken coop was repaired and Horacio the rooster guarded his flock with a ferociousness that guaranteed him a place on the chopping block. A swing was added to the weeping willow tree. After school, prepubescent boys would slide into the yard on their bikes and swing under the willow tree as they watched the girls grooming their ponies. The rusted, corroded iron covering the old well had been stripped off and the rotting siding removed and replaced, all made safe so the windmill could spin and clang again, drawing water to pump and store in the tank on the hill. The slow rate of repair-and-replace made it clear to whoever was watching from the farm trucks that drove by that a budget was necessary.

Jess had chosen his time carefully. Like any hunter, he had watched and learned our routines. Walter was often away for long days and nights, and driving to San Francisco on the BMW bike—before the arrival of the Saab—he could make it to American Zoetrope on Folsom Street in fifty-two minutes. When the children were at school, I was alone. Jess was the quiet patriarch of his family, staying close to the ranch. Had he decided to come down on his own after seeing us at those Pancake Breakfasts? Or had he decided after one of their family kitchen-table discussions about the changes in town? I was known by his three sons and Lydia, his sister-in-law, and maybe some passing remarks helped him think I just might be someone to help.

From the kitchen window, I saw Jess as he slowly got out of the truck, carefully closing the cab door, and looking around, taking it all in—what we had done and what was yet to do. He knocked on the back door, still the same in years when he might have come in with a greeting but no need for a knock.

"Come in, Jess. A cup of coffee?"

He nodded and followed me into the kitchen, again taking in the old familiarities and the few changes. Some fresh American perk came quietly to a brew.

Jess sat down at the table, and I brought over the coffee, mugs, and sugar, and joined him. We spoke of neighborly things, and I waited for a while.

"Is there something I can do for you, Jess?"

Only then did he reach into the inside pocket of his waist-coat to bring out some several-times-folded papers and place them on the table between us.

I knew to be slow, cautious, and unhurried, and didn't turn them around or pick them up to see what he had brought. I looked at Jess as he now held his coffee cup with one hand, and waited for him to tell me this story.

He unfolded the papers carefully onto the table, running his fingers over them to smooth out the creases. He spoke softly, as he would to a foaling mare or while settling a milk cow in her stall, as he began to explain his situation. He had a few thoroughbred and papered mares that he had picked up from the stockyard, where a familiarity and companionship among the ranchers brought deals along with comfort. It was not unknown for broken-down thoroughbred horses from the weekend's racing at the Santa Rosa track to be unloaded at the stockyard just south of Petaluma for the Monday sales. It would be a quick turnover, most going to the slaughterhouses, but a few thoroughbreds would be looked over and gathered up by the canny or gambling rancher looking to make a few dollars. Some would pick up old papered studs to be held in yards around the racetracks, others would pick up a mare or two, and some would trailer both back to their ranches. Jess might have been among the latter, as now there were yearlings that needed to be registered before the January first deadline if he was to get the best dollar for them.

Which is where I came in. Jess's first and family language was Portuguese. He was the last of his generation to absorb English through his children and extended family. Much of the stockyard talk was in Portuguese and Spanish, while church Latin embraces them all. His voice was still soft as his fingers moved across the forms and he guided me. I picked up the pen and slowly, following his directions for each of the colts, filled in the markings on the drawings and the breeding details. Did the colts have names? I can't remember, but we might have had to fill those in, too. When we were done, I pushed the papers back across the table for him to check. He didn't look at them again. He had watched me work and now folded them back along their old creases and put the papers back into his vest pocket once more.

Jess lingered a little with the cup between his hands, sitting quietly and taking me in up close, seeing and settling within himself that with the grade mare thriving and happy, the farmhouse full of children, and the wood-burning stove working in the kitchen, I would care for this farmhouse that had belonged to his friend, Manuel Peters, and assented it would be fine for us to call it home.

Ben's Barn

The Tacherra Ranch is a school bus stop and an easy walk from the houses on the mesa. There were pens and fields for the ponies while some lucky families had quarter-to-half-acre yards of their own to fence. Ben Meyer lived in a trailer, tucked into the base of the Francisco Mesa that crested across and over Phinney's Hill. The ranch barn had escaped a fire that took out the farmhouse in 1972, but remained bruised and shaken. Moving from the Randall Ranch at the top of 13 Turns after it had been swallowed by the Golden Gate National Recreation Area, Ben trucked in his trailer to resettle and caretake another's land, closer to town. Ben's Barn, as it quickly became known, was across the road from us, nestled into the south side of the hill. His trailer was protected, parked in a swale in front of the large old barn. The barn remains to this day a monument to times past and times present, living on in its incarnation as the Peace Barn. I'm thinking there were five, but remembering four strong Swiss children, Fritz, Buck, Meitty, and Heidi. One summer, their mother swung by for a brief visit. Meeting her while sitting at the tiny table in the trailer, sipping the bittersweet coffee of Ben's preparing, I saw a beautiful yet worn lady who seemed to have sidestepped this hillbilly life into another of her choosing. Neither she nor Ben showed the height that Fritz and Meitty carried.

Riding a pony down through the eucalyptus grove to Ben's Barn or the beach, or both, was the biggest, best adventure for pony-loving children. And the ponies: Flame, Flicker, Dusty, Daisy, Cinnamon, and Pony-Boy, enjoyed their charges, the adventures, the care—and they knew when and where to trot or to gallop or to amble. Treats came from pockets, the grocery store, and the grain bin. It was as good a life for the ponies as for their young riders. They felt wild, and yet were safe. Finishing his morning school and trucking rounds by the time school ended in the afternoon, Ben would be out and around the barn, able to find a piece of tack here, or tie a knot there. Then, as the day wore on, he could retire to the trailer, letting the girls come in and find him, even sitting crouched close together on the old sofa that later would become someone's bed. There was coffee on the hob, cigarette butts in overflowing saucers, and maybe even soda pop and Velveeta cheese in the trailer's tiny kitchen fridge. There was electricity strung on precarious wires to sheds and the barn beyond. And there was talk, man talk and horse talk, and even machine talk for the growing adolescent boys who came to be there too. Mostly the talk was single-syllabled but of a steadying nature; it was a comfort to young children who didn't know they needed comfort. Ben had an eye for children as well as horses, and saw more than he spoke about. He watched and didn't interfere.

Always an outsider, he held himself aloof from all but those families, neither cowboys nor ranchers, who held familial memories of such a life. Middleton, O'Conner, Kostelic were men of his understanding but for the rest, he rubbed along as best as he had a mind to. John O'Conner was another quiet man, seemingly gentle on his horses, his family, and the children, and a friend to Ben. Both Ben and John were safe havens for girls with more ponies than parents. John worked with the girls, showing those who would and could learn to rope and barrel race. The families knit together as they slid daughters and horses, sons and machines, between each other, teaching skills along the way to anyone who could grasp them.

When we first came to Peters Dairy, Ben didn't think much of me, though he could easily see that while Babe had been someone's castoff, she had become my much-beloved mare. But with an English saddle and snaffle bridle—and a farm, not a ranch—he dismissed me to a place of low standing. He watched and waited for me to come to him. For he knew I would. There would be a time when I would need something and then he could do me the favor.

But I did have two things going for me. As a tall woman, I could be seen moving through my life by Meitty, as she struggled with her limbs and body growing longer than she had any right to expect, and watching me could bring her a molecule of hope through adolescence. Ben liked to see his girls well mounted, and Meitty was a natural-born horsewoman. Ben had found a great dun cow pony that was a fantastic barrel racer and carried her well. As I admired them both, Ben softened a little.

He held a tight rein on his girls but one day, after school, he let Meitty ride out with me. It was a hard and fast ride, up through the back pastures, past the Tacherra Ranch, turning up the hill by the water tanks, onto the high ridge before heading down the forest trail to Dogtown, the gully of Rancho Baulines and home before supper, taking Meitty further afield than she had ever gone before. It thrilled her.

Occasionally, I would also need a babysitter, which meant easy and good money close to home. Kind, gentle Meitty, and occasionally Heidi too, proved to be perfect companions for our children. Our brood loved the excitement of real cowgirls, and the girls loved the warmth and clear space of the farmhouse. We were physically close and safe enough that neither Ben nor I had to worry.

As high school claimed the older girls, they moved away from their ponies, but not away from the barn. There was familial safety yet adventure there as Ben's boys revved up their motorbikes to drive up and down, up and down the flats. Jobs were needed. Local waitressing claimed the more cautious girls; the gas station, mechanics, and trucking for Ben's boys. But Ben could read the town's shifting. The siblings in the Tacherra family, who owned the Fransisco Ranch, were jostling amongst themselves, and a land sale would become inevitable. Ben had been around long enough to know how this would play out, and when a ranch in Sonoma became available to him, he took the months needed to trailer out. Horses, family, and, one day, the old house-trailer they lived in had all moved on. Their final home was on the corner where Highway 116 died, splitting into 121 and sliding into 12, both weaving their way up into Napa.

Even though it was a summer day when I stopped by, the dark and the dust made the kitchen gloom seem cold. Ben sat in the kitchen, alone, with his coffee. The family had already scattered, as if by shotgun, blasted out of the sunlight of Bolinas and scrambling for the knife-edge of existence where they could hold on and move forward. Buck took to the skies in delicate aircraft and would fly over us all on sunny Sundays before he returned, making a home and family in town.

Not too long before he left, Ben rode Roan down to our farm. Sitting relaxed on the gelding, fully tacked with his rope beside the saddle horn, as if this was the last ride he would take. Roan was a big, splendid Appaloosa who carried his ancestral history proudly. He looked to have been a good roping horse in his day, though we rarely saw that. Ben held lightly to his image and rarely sullied it with proof of any kind. What did Ben come down to say or to hear? For me to look up at him and tell him again what a fine horse Roan was? Maybe that was all he needed to hear, that I knew he and his horse were champs.

Ribbons Galore

When Steve Aikenhead was the math teacher and school librarian at the Bolinas-Stinson Unified School District, he corralled parents and teachers, gathering us together to write, as honestly as we could, a picture of our time and experiences at the school. Some of us were by then wondering if it might be nice to write something as we came up for air from the daily rounds of overflowing kitchens, scruffy kids, smelly socks, and endless meetings. Steve had researched the school's scant written history and tracked down the still-living retired teachers, coaxing, tempting them to share how it was—back then, back when—allowing them to put any record straight. *Group Memories: School Days in Bolinas and Stinson Beach* was published on January 1, 1993.

The history of a school is a snapshot of the community it serves, as it was when written. What Steve did, as many historians do, was go back far enough that he and we could see how and when the education patterns of a community changed. Who held the power, who set the course and direction of education? Then there were the rumors, stories, and myths that became history to incorporate, or not. Who was the young fourth-grader who would arrive at school with a bag of marijuana to share with the older boys and thereby learn the art of bartering, trade, and, possibly, debt collection, all of which could come under the heading of social studies or even math skills? As new parents came into the school with different goals and ideas, school board meetings could become disruptive, even physical, with tables taking the brunt of the abuse. But different voices were clamoring to be heard. As the '60s rolled over to the '70s, many parents were asking what had happened to the three Rs.

It could have been 1974 or 1975 when three of us horse-riding moms offered to teach an after-school semester class in horsemanship for the fifth through eighth grades. The curriculum of the school was adventuresome and, in retrospect, awesome. Harriet Kossman was building and leading a team of artists into an exciting arts program. Dave Duffin was running a motorcycle shop for the boys to learn to hold steady, let loose, and stay focused. The grounding and inspiration of these teachers gave many children who entered their orbit a way to tread with courage along their life paths. The liberal school board, thinking we horse-loving mothers had finally seen the errors of our rigid ways, willingly approved of our program. For the next semester, these lessons were scheduled to be held after school hours and off campus. Sixteen young girls scuffed and shuffled the quarter-mile down the road to Blackberry Farm. Bumping together, clustered, scared to be the first one to arrive, they made it up the driveway and entered through our wide-open front door to shyly crowd into the living room. They were intrigued but, like a herd of yearlings let loose together for the first time, skittish, stepping into this new ground in the big white farmhouse they walked past every day. We introduced ourselves, Susie, Linda, and Aggie, and asked them each to do the same; to tell us their name, school grade, and the name of their pony.

It was in this class setting that Carrie and Connie, aged ten and eleven, first came into our lives. While the state of California in its courtroom paper-shuffling wisdom decided their fate, they were tucked like wild butterflies into this bouquet of young girls, flitting from one family to another, gathering nectar from day to day, week to week.

After the introductions, each child was given a piece of paper and a pencil, and asked to write a little bit about their ponies. Two or three ponies were shared but still, they all had ponies to ride. The next hour was agony for some of those girls and, after they handed their papers in (to be corrected and returned), we saw why. Only two or three had scribbled nonstop and turned over the page, while others could barely manage a scant two sentences. And so ended the first lesson in ridin', readin', 'ritin', and 'rithmatic. This was going to be an interesting semester. And it was fun too, for them and for us. Along with the four Rs came cookies and conversations, games and lessons in equestrian good manners, leading, we hoped, to an awareness of responsibility for their ponies and each other. There were field trips to other ranches like the O'Conners', showing different ways of caring for horses, always with more cookies. As the semester ended in June and the summer vacation beckoned, we held their first annual horse show and gymkhana at Rancho Baulines. The children were still shy and skittish, while we were terrified that we had asked too much of them and they would not show up. Only a couple had signed in early.

The fog was still low on the ground at 8 a.m. when we put up a sign and balloons and opened the ranch gate. As the morning began, Janet Robbins, another English mother now living in Inverness, came down to help. She arrived with her bemused screenwriter husband Matthew, Walter's oldest friend from Johns Hopkins, and then the USC film school, to give Walter some moral support. Then, as the sun began to push aside the rising fog, we saw the first slow movement of ponies in twos and threes coming up the long driveway, as children, ponies, and parents began to arrive. For many of them, this was the first time they had brought their ponies beyond the town's enclosure, to ride the mile or so to where the road out of town met Highway 1 and where the imposing Rancho Baulines sat in splendor, a marker on the road. As they came to where we were sitting at an old picnic table, our clipboards and pens at the ready to sign them in, they also saw the box of ribbons lying under the table and dared to become excited as they finally realized this day was for them. Janet guided them along, taking the dollar bills, assigning rider numbers, and adding names to class entries. The entry fees had been set at $2 but now, on the day, it was upped to $2.50. Money went into the tin, ponies and riders went into the riding arena, and parents hung onto the rails, watching their darlings stepping up and trotting out with nerves and pride jostling together in equal measure. Horseback riding was no longer just a way to pass the time after school. These young riders now carried a new level of caring and engagement with their ponies. More parents arrived, clutching buckets and halters, as instructed by their children, along with the children's cakes and cookies baked for the bake sale. These were to be judged by Lydia Tacherra, and for Lydia to come off her ranch and onto another was a serious endorsement; she did not move far from her home, her mother's house on the property at the top of Phinney's Hill. But Lydia welcomed us all into her orbit, caring for little ones as their mothers, striking out on their own as teachers or nurses or farmers, needed her help. Lydia was a matriarchal backbone of the community on whom we could lean and expand. She spent a lot of time judging the cakes before giving out another blue ribbon to the winner, Beth Ball. Only now could the cakes and cookies be sold and eaten.

As the day continued, we felt a silent wonderment and satisfaction, watching the Western and English riders come together. The older girls from Ben's barn who had been too cool to come to our class rode over. Watching at first, they began to see and hear what they could do and cautiously put their dollars down and joined in. Surely, they could win the barrel racing and sit-a-buck events, collect a ribbon, and keep their cool. On the promise of all-they-could-eat food for free, four seventh- and eighth-grade boys biked in to move poles, hay bales, and jumps. They too could look cool and leave little hearts pattering. There was a raffle, with prizes donated by whoever from the town said yes. There were Western and English classes and barely a hard hat in view, though we insisted they be worn for the jumping classes. Due to the Bolinas Volunteer Fire Department's presence and beer-selling activities, the Men's Beer and Bra Race was a lively finale.

As the sun came out at the end of the day, we packed up and cleared everything away from the field behind the ranch and went home. Was it tea or beer or both that was served at the kitchen table while Susie, Linda, and I opened the box and counted the dollars? Yes, there was enough to pay for the day's insurance and Doc Lapkin for the ribbons. No child had gone home without a ribbon, though many had been appropriated by proud hipster fathers to hook into their worn leather belts. There were a few ribbons left over, lying like wallflowers in the box to linger in a cupboard before eventually fading away. But not in memory. That first school semester and little horse show birthed a small riding club, then the Marin County Pony Club that continues, through clever metamorphosis, to this day.

Then, following along, as dreams can, in 1982 Jack and Mary Siedman held the first Bolinas Stinson School annual track and field day. Even with Jack on the school board, it took a while for this idea to be totally accepted. Hiring Anthony Stewart as a full-time PE teacher was one of the best thing that Jack ever did. And the track-and-field day remains a glorious end to the school year.

And for us, the farm, our family, and our hearts were filled. As that summer ended, Carrie and Connie came to live with us. While more than one friend asked Walter what on Earth we were doing, he never questioned my path or wavered in his support. He understood the grief I carried with my inability to have more children. Maybe it was an unspoken truth that I needed the sisters as much as they needed us.

The arrival of Carrie and Connie into the family, with a room of their own and joining the routines of farm chores, family meals (with desserts), homework, and curfews, brought the seemly manageable family of two children to the definitely joyously chaotic farm full of four—plus friends.

* * *

Paul Hirsch wrote his tender account of the Droid Olympics in an article for *CineMontage* and quotes Walter saying:

"In June of '78, [it was 1976] *my wife Aggie had put on a horse show for the local kids in Bolinas,"* Murch continued. *"And I was eyeing the ribbons and trophies when the idea came to me to throw a similar event for the assistant editors on Apocalypse Now, to celebrate their skills."*

Eyeing—nothing—this was serious envy!

Like the fathers who had proudly worn their daughters' bright colorful ribbons on their belts, the ribbons stirred lust in Walter's heart. Not one to abscond with any of his family's ribbons (he would never have survived the attempt), it took two years for him to figure out how to get one of his own. And that was how The Droid Olympics, a decathlon of film-editing skills, was born.

Those three brief summer days, one in 1978, during *Apocalypse Now;* then 1982 with *Return to Oz, Dragonslayer,* and *Black Stallion Returns;* and finally, in 1987 with *The Unbearable Lightness of Being,* we gathered the mostly post-production crews into teams for battle. The fluid film community of Bay Area productions was drawn together and put out to pasture onto the farm and into our home. Sunshine was in short supply in post-production suites and buildings.

But there were practicalities to be taken care of. Was there time to visit Doc Lapkin in Novato, bringing him a two-frame clip of film and trying to explain to him what it is and ask for it to be the centerpiece of the ribbons? His storefront was one door from the old Novato cinema. There was a bar squeezed in between them.

"Why, I've never seen anything like that before."

"Only blue, Doc. They only want to win. Coming in second doesn't count with this crowd. And can you put 'The Droid Olympics' in the surround?"

"What the heck is that, then? I'll have them for you in two weeks."

Doc was in the middle of the summer and autumn horse-show and rodeo season. Of course, he had them ready and was still smiling and "kinda proud" as I thanked him and walked out carrying a box of twelve blue ribbons and a bowling trophy that now held a frame of film for the Super Droid of the Day.

The new Ford truck worked overtime as Walter set about *borrowing* editing equipment from the city, and I drove in the other direction for straw bales to be brought in from Tobies to set out on what has never managed to become a lawn.

"We cannot afford to feed all those people. It has to be a potluck. Maybe we can ask Jack and Chuck Oakander to bring their split oil drums down and fire up a barbecue." The brothers not only brought their oil drums, but (though maybe I am dreaming or imagining) even oysters. Everybody brought food and drinks with enough to share. It was a wonderful affirmation of all that is best in American country living.

The four children were getting seriously excited. This was a grown-up party, and they all had important chores to do and parts to play. Carrie was handed a clipboard; her task was to keep track of who was entering what event. She handled a near-impossible job with great tenacity, standing her ground and pointing out who was cheating and when.

"What is going on over there?" Like our Pony Club horse shows, the Droid Olympics took place in full view of anyone on the road. Passersby would casually saunter in to sit, sip a beer, and while away an hour on a Sunday afternoon. There was no comparable exchange of events, though; remembering back, we tried to tie some in. Naturally, Walter had come up with some interesting names for the events, known only to those droids living in the dark caves of cinematic post-production hallways. Both days ended in the hyper madness of exhaustion with the pony show's beer-and-bra race turning to the trims-and-outs dash.

To be a Super Droid and hold up that bowling trophy gave weeks and months of delight and laughter in the dark booths of the editorial suites growing in the Bay Area. Somewhere out there are three—shelved and dusty, maybe even boxed away—but, hopefully, not yet thrown out.

* * *

Horse barns and boarding stables become their own communities with shared responsibility for each other and our horses. The barns were not unlike the houseboat community we had left behind where we all watched out for one another, checking where ropes were tied fast in a storm so boats were not swinging fast and loose. Horses could also get loose, hurt, or in trouble, and whoever was around helped. Extra feed, tack, or medicine was freely shared, and adults and children worked together for and with one another.

We were not alone. Just along the coastal shoreline, sliding off Highway 101, there were trails leading from the horse stables at Tennessee Valley, following a coastal trail up and down to Muir Beach, then over Mount Tamalpais to Bolinas, which held Ben's Barn, the Tacherra Ranch, Blackberry Farm, Rancho Baulines, and, later, Vanishing Point Ranch. Taking either the valley or the ridge trails north another eleven miles dropped you into Point Reyes Station and Willow Ridge Barn behind the town of Point Reyes. And that was just on the coast. More stables inland held the companionship and freedom found in the company of horses.

All these barns were connected geographically, but in those early years it was with Tink Pervier's barn in Muir Beach that we shared the most. Tink and I, both mothers from England, held the firm belief that young children needed as much fresh air and exercise as they did classroom time, and that for us, ponies were obviously a necessary part of that time. Freedom for us—for them—was riding; we couldn't get our children out far and fast enough into the hills. Being closer to San Francisco, visible from the tiny Muir Beach cove, Tink had more to contend with in terms of interference. She got harassed from all sides: the city folks getting away from the city but not wanting to really get close to the countryside, conservative environmentalists who hassled her for anything that they didn't think was "natural," and the bureaucracy of county management that really didn't know what they were managing or for whom. We didn't talk a lot about it, each having our own struggles, but it must have been hard for Tink. Her closest ally was George Wheelwright, an Englishman who had sold land to the Zen Center. He also understood the importance of letting young people explore the hills. Memories are made from childhood roaming, and such memories can call you to love and protect them forever.

At about the same time as we held our first little horse show, Tink held hers in a field along the winding road to Muir Woods. It was mowed, roped, and set up in the same makeshift manner as ours, but to us, it all looked very spiffy that day. Horse trailers came in from Tennessee Valley, San Geronimo Valley, and even further north. But for us, the mountain road from Stinson to Muir Beach was too intimidating. Climbing, twisting, and on the edge of the coastline, with vertical to the ocean below, it seemed too dangerous a road for hauling horses.

Who was it that first said, "Let's ride it"? And once said, the idea would not go away. For already, on a weekly basis, as runaway mothers, two or three of us took to those hills at a mad gallop, stealing the time to still make it home before our children returned from school.

"It's only a few hours. We can ride, take the children. Their parents can meet us there and take them home after their ponies are settled." This was the adventure we had hoped for those children. We set out, choosing the easiest of the hidden trails that climbed up to the ridge from Rancho Baulines. Once on the ridge, it was two or three hours of gentle, ambling riding in the shaded trails, through the forested hills, and into the bright sunshine on the plains. There were trees to name, birds disturbed by our intrusion scolding us, and, in the sunshine and meadows, young hands would reach out so fingers could caress and slide through the tall grasses. Drifting and dreaming, enjoying and trusting their ponies like never before, the children were quiet while we watched over them on the trail, leading and tailing, encompassing them until finally dipping down through the heather plantation into the field below. The ponies were happy too, with the fresh trails and full hay nets for the night. Parents drove back and forth over the coast road firmly in harness to their children's needs; the next day, families gathered again, bundled against the coastal fog, watching as their children rode in this other show. Two days was enough for them, and, after putting the ponies away safely for the night, parents bundled up the children with their new memories and ribbons, and took them home.

Monday was often a quiet, solitary day for those left behind, when menfolk left for work and children were at school. We were happy to leave the laundry on the floor, hitch a ride over the mountain into Muir Beach. Then, we shared a quick coffee of gratitude with Tink before tacking up the horses, haltering the ponies and heading back over the hill through the morning fog across the ridge and down to our hometown again.

Lydia Tacherra Grand Mother:
August 18, 1927 - November 21, 1995

On Saturday, November 25, 1995, the sun shone brightly
into the Catholic church at the foot of Horseshoe Hill. Lydia
Tacherra lay smiling in state in the center of the church, surrounded by her family and community. After the service, she
was laid to rest overlooking the land where she had grown up,
married, raised her children, lived out her life as an elder, and
died. Her brother-in-law Jesse pulled the bell rope as he had
done for over seventy years, summoning us all to the base of
Horseshoe Hill as the time-honored Catholic Mass began. In
the spirit of the times, the younger menfolk from her family
spoke of their remembrances and the meaning of Lydia's life for
them, but it was the women of Portugal who prayed over her
and acknowledged her beauty and sisterhood, and Susan, the
niece-in-law Lydia had embraced from the East Coast, who sang
the loving lament.

Born and raised in her mother's Bolinas house, Lydia
Francisco married Alfred Tacherra, raised her own two girls on
their ranch, and remained to die on that land. The Franciscos
were one of the Portuguese families to come from the Azores, an
island that existed by farming and fishing, and so Lydia knew,
beyond the bones of her being, the value of land. Not as we
value it today, mainly as dollars per acre, but what living and
working the land gives and does for the human condition. Lydia
was a child of the generation that settled in Bolinas in the early
1890s and inherently knew the intrinsic worth of the haven they
had created here. Growing up and working the land, she learned
on what day to sow seed and what day to reap the harvest. She
also instinctively knew about people and, as a woman of her
character, was never embarrassed to speak her mind. What she

cared most about was the land, the church, the family, and the community. When her family moved to sell their ranch, Lydia resisted. She fought with the strength of a woman who knows she is right beyond the law, with the force of one who has nothing to lose by the fighting, and so, in the end, she won her place in all our hearts as she fought for her birthright as she saw it, within her family and her community.

In the early 1970s, when we, as a new wave of immigrants, came to Bolinas to make this our home, Lydia was a middle-aged farming matron. For those of Lydia's generation, we were at the least a nuisance and, at worst, a serious threat to the status quo, but we didn't faze Lydia, who took each of us fairly as she found us. Lydia accepted us all, whether we came from old countries with old country ways, had fled from the cities with no ways at all, or had moved quietly from one part of the US to another. She knew that as young mothers who were trying to raise our families and farm the land, our commitment to the community would follow as predictably as eight chicks would emerge from thirteen eggs under a setting hen. All she had to do was sit on us for a while, then gently guide those of us who emerged. With an old-world courtesy that gave credence to our lives as women, farmers, and mothers, she did just that.

Lydia came to the first horse shows we held at Rancho Baulinas in 1976. Whatever it took for us to be committed to the community, Lydia backed a hundred percent, and for that, the women of Bolinas are forever grateful. We didn't realize until she died that by her example of strength within the bonds of family, Lydia gave those of us who wanted to take it our matriarchy.

It was already dusk and a soft rain had begun to fall when, returning home at the end of that Saturday, I stopped at the stop sign by Las Baulinas Nursery. The backhoe, driven by Lydia's nephew Bill, now finished with his work at the church, came rumbling down the road and I slowly followed him home. It is said that before she became ill, Lydia saw a mountain lion on the Francisco Mesa. I am sure it was a lioness who came to take her place, and watch over us in the years ahead.

Chapter 5

A Farm Friday

This year's savings was spent taking down the back row of eucalyptus to a height of fifteen to twenty feet. I was looking for an early bee swarm and found one eucalyptus tree down. Chuck's tree crew is a great team, and we got a lot of farm and garden tidying done. I hope we don't have to do that row anymore. Granny had an expression she used to say entering the last few years of her life: "That will see me out." I always hope the big pruning will see us out. But then, suddenly, the need to do it again happens in a new year. Now, if I had to put windbreak trees in again, what would I use? I don't think it would be eucalyptus. The blackberries are returning to the depth they were when we first came here forty-two years ago, and I realize that however much I work on them, they will find a way to stay.

Today, I took on the house and kitchen compost bin. I managed to get half of the bin into a full wheelbarrow, loaded down with rich black compost. It is beautiful. Truly, the richness of the garden is found in the deep, dark soil. Sifting through the soil, I unearthed, literally, the blue knobbed teaspoon, a small brown teapot, one-third of the remains of Bea's St. Nicholas School Panama hat, and my old garden knife with half of the wooden handle eaten away. A few months ago, Walter TY had pulled an old felt-tip pen from the compost. It still works!

"Must be from the 1970s," he says, but that cannot be. I would have used that compost up. But things do get pushed about and show up ages later. Still, one wonders what is in that pen ink that it is still working thirty-some years later.

Who will find the aquamarine ring that my mother-in-law, Katharine, gave me the first Christmas after we were married? We were going out; I was dressed up and in a hurry. It slipped off my finger as I tossed Lemon Kick's hay into the stall for his evening feed. I don't even remember if I noticed right away that the ring was gone. Lemon Kick was hungry and we were late. That was forty years ago. How does that happen?

The new soil all went into the bee and black currant bury-patch bed, which is weeded and tidied. The bin is now set straight again beside the chicken coop. The chickens loved the work and quickly pecked away, feasting on sow bugs and spare worms.

Not to be outdone, Mitzi caught another good-sized gopher, but was cross that the bathroom door was shut. She went around and around the house with the gopher until the door was open. She left the gallbladder and one foot. Always one foot.

Fresh bright-green grass is bursting up, the two arable fields sprouting fava ground cover while the two smaller pasture grass fields are slower, shy in their blooming. On my bike ride, another eucalyptus tree has been called and has fallen into the lagoon, sinking like a floundering deer.

The small narcissus minor daffodils that continue to welcome us every spring are fading now, always emerging in time for St. Valentine's Day and heralding spring's awakening. The wild plum trees are blooming; next, it will be the turn of the greengage plum. The young wild bracken fronds are a bright, light green and still tightly curled, ready to welcome an early spring along the roadside.

I go out to pick six stalks of glistening chard for my lunch and the last of the daffodils to put in Bea's bedroom. She is back for two nights and then flies 'home' to Buenos Aires. I have to remember my words: This is the farm. Bea is gone. Buenos Aires is her home.

Cannes Calling

The Cannes, Venice, and Locarno film festivals have a common heritage that, despite the business occurring in their hotel lobbies, bars, and dark restaurants, gives each festival a unique place in cinematic history. Begun in 1932, the Venice festival is the oldest, but after the Second World War, an idea, maybe tossed about at a meal in a screening room, became molded into a collaboration from the cultural bodies of those cities to combine, through the art of cinema, the cultural heritage of the new post war age. Today, Locarno still holds a strong festival but it is not counted as one of the big three. Berlin, eager to become a part of cultural healing, moved into that place.

Phil Kaufman's film for HBO, *Hemingway & Gellhorn*—which could have been called Gellhorn & Hemingway and that Walter had edited—had been accepted at the 2012 Cannes festival. HBO is stepping up into the film business as Amazon, Netflix, and Apple begin their assault on cinemas. They are the new brash boys in town, elbowing old brick-and-mortar studios aside as they clamor for deals and sales. The festivals are showcases for their new productions and there is a constant hustle with producers and distributors pretending they are no Harvey Weinstein, while all behaving as badly as they can get away with. In the lobbies of old hotels and in the beachfront restaurants, there are meetings oiled with the good food and wine that Cannes lays before them.

While Phil must attend those meetings, he needs Walter to be on hand for the things that go sideways at screenings, and the sweetener was that they will pay for me to go too. The hyper-madness that is Cannes is offset by the tender intimate moments at the cafés and late-night dining with friends under May's spring emerging.

We fell under the festival's spell in 1971, the first time we went to an alternate festival celebrating non-mainstream commercial work. Though *THX-1138* was being released commercially, it was rightly seen as non-mainstream. Then, in 1974, there was the delight of kindness from the owner of the little pension giving us a magical stay with *The Conversation*, before the insanity of *Apocalypse Now* in 1979. The sweetness of being with Janet Leigh in 1998, working away in her eighties with *Touch of Evil*. Then came *Apocalypse Now Redux* in 2001. *Hemingway & Gellhorn* would be our sixth trip and could be the last time we enjoy such an adventure. With the beautiful spring season, the harvests of fish and fruit, every trip to Cannes has given us memories where friendships are reinforced, tightened with the fisherman's knot of this last application of devotion to the work. The moonlight is warm, the cherries are bountiful, and the seafood is fresh. I'm smiling at my willingness to go. It will be fun to travel again with Phil Kaufman and his family, even knowing this is all work for Walter.

The alarm is set for 3 a.m. as Walter must go to the Grand Palais to check out the sound system and speakers and run the first reel of the film. We walk along the Croisette and find our way to the back of a big circus tent. There are thick cables taped to the ground to watch out for and a maze of black swing curtains to weave through before coming to the front stage of this three-thousand-seat theater. The night-shift festival crew is cleaning up from the last screening and preparing for the next show, which is *H&G*. Nicole Kidman and Clive Owen will be sparkling alongside Phil. The night-shift gaffer crew has seen the Walters of the world through the years and, in their French way, accept his presence and his request to see and hear the first reel of the film. The sound levels, the sync, and focus all could do with adjusting, but the projectionist and crew stand and shrug and say "it is not possible," or "only this much." So, for this screening, the last months of work are crushed by the projectionist, who always has the last cut. Walter is dejected but not surprised. He has been in this position before and must now share his assessment with Phil. Despite their cringing apprehension, the screening goes well; they have done almost all they can do for the film and now it, like all work before it, must stand on its own.

The next day, there is no lingering, and we pack our bags. Walter returns to New York and Mark Levinson's *Particle Fever*, and I return to the farm, where a full summer of work and community life is waiting. There is a fundraising golf tournament to organize for KWMR radio, the annual Pony Club show to announce, and the farm to focus on as best I can.

Bees

It was a Saturday afternoon when I arrived back to the farm and quickly unpacked and began to settle in again. By noon on Sunday, bee buddy and supreme sound guy Pete Horner had brought my new package of bees over from the Marin Beekeeping Group. These are Italian bees, sweet and gentle and the only bees I need now. I have come to accept that beekeeping is a hobby. I do it for fun and spend far too many dollars on it to enjoy—or not—the fruits of my labors. We got lucky on Sunday, with a day's break between rains. Luckier than we both deserved, as it turned out, as neither of us was as prepared as we should have been. My hive frames had been left outside and got wet and there was mold all over the wax sheets. But we managed to get the yellow bee box together. Walter TY brought out the old chopping board, so the hive now sat up higher on chunks of discarded fencing, a disused kitchen drawer, and my old chopping board. We were not very good—rather clumsy, in fact—but the bees were gentle and kind to us and we got them all in. There was a little bit of honey left on an old comb. Pete used his key to remove the seal on the tin and we put in the sugar water. Then we put the queen in—all backwards, really. We didn't remember the proper way to do it until we were finished with the two hives in the orchard and having lunch in the kitchen.

Then we knew. Set the hive up first. Remove five to six frames, take out the honey tin. Set the queen in her cage securely in the frames. Wallop the bees out of the box and put the frames back. Cover with spacer. (I put mine on the next morning.) We have decided that feeding tins at the front of the hive are better than over the top board. (But months later, I find that both methods have their problems.)

Pete needed a bottom board, and we found an extra one in the shed that I was able to give him. He went home and got his bees in before dark.

The next morning, I went out and put on an inner cover and brushed away the dead bees I had squashed. Too many, in my carelessness, and I am sorry for the extra work for the bees.

The bees in the yellow garden hive had all left the travel box and moved into their hive. There were two small clumps of new bees still clinging to the back of the box. Most of them had died from not finding their way into the hive, but I banged them all out anyway, letting them rest on the dead brown eucalyptus leaves lying in front of the hive. Those that were alive and not too tired were able to find their way into their new hive home over the next hour or two. Like moving into a college dormitory, those already settling in have grabbed the best spots, clumped in the two center frames, covering the queen, who is still in her box. They need to be all safely in before a new storm takes hold. It has begun now, and it will rain all day.

Every spring, I try to get ahead of the bees' needs, and fail. Somehow it is impossible to be as prepared as I should be and it ends up being closer to summer than spring when the boxes and bees are set up. I went out into the shed for another hour, which quickly became two, building frames for the hive bodies. Now all the double hive bodies are ready, and I have one more hive body ready and waiting for a swarm. Well, it isn't ready yet, but it is ready to get ready. It is nice to bang away in the shed with a mug of tea on the bench beside me, getting dusted with wax and goodness-knows-what as I patch up the frame bodies, scrape off the old wax, and fit them with lovely white comb start. The new frames look so pristine and hopeful and optimistic. There is no way the bees could not like them. In fact, the bees are already checking my work, finding little scraps of honey among the old wax and taking it back, to where? The newly refreshed old hive may be where, but because of the not-yet-done weeding around their hive, the bees have already learned to fly up and out of their hive rather than in a straight line forward. These bees are gentle around me and have drunk all their sugar water. I went to check the orchard hives and their jars are still half full. Now they are submerged in the bursting apple blossom that is waiting to greet them.

After three very hot days in May, the heat wave broke, though I need to water what I can. On Thursday the yellow hive bees were outside of their hive. I worried that they were going to swarm, but it turned out that another batch of brood had hatched and was on a school outing, learning the lay of the land. I spend another hour in the shed, banging more bee supers together, and slopped yellow paint on one to go out when it is dry. One super will carry cut comb and I'm going to try to keep cut-and-spun honey separately. But I don't have much luck with a straight comb. It is tricky to put in. I'm doing something wrong, or not doing something I should be doing. While I was going through the old combs, I found some honey and brought it in. Two and a half pounds. I kept eating chunks of comb while putting it into the trays. I will finish prepping two more supers and take them out to the orchard hives on Friday.

The early morning was sunny and warm, and the wind was still not up by 10:30, which gave the bees more time to forage. We work them differently here by the coast than inland. Each geography with its unique microclimate charts the rhythms of work. Often there is no midday sun when the bees are all out, so this early-morning time can be good. I went into all the beehives today and got my first sting from the yellow hive. She didn't get deep; the stinger stuck in my glove. It is a good first for the season. This home hive is roaring along and I put on another honey super, this one for comb honey, and I am excited to see what will happen. One new hive in the orchard is not quite so strong, though the queen seems to be laying nice patterns of brood. Maybe she was just a little slow getting started. I added another hive body to it anyway. The two-year-old hive in the orchard is also strong. The bees are storing honey in the super and not putting in brood, as far as I can see. I have already made another super for them and will add it on in a couple of weeks. The old orchard hive looks like it needs no help from me! There is brood and honey in the second hive body and, try as I might, I could not lift it off to check the lower hive. So I left it. I will make up a super for honey and add that next week.

The youngest hive in the orchard has no brood at all. I found two queen cells, one still capped and the other open. I will check again next weekend and see if there is brood, or if the other queen cell has opened. There are some scatterings of brood cells in the other young hive and not much honey, maybe eight pounds in the added super. Is the honey flow over for a while? Do the bees need more water?

There has been a lot of wind again this last week. Short bursts of wind, sharp and angry, with one day of rain on Thursday. It was cold the day after I added the second hive bodies and supers. The bees were sitting at the hive entrance. At first, I thought they were cross, thinking about swarming out of there. Then I thought maybe they are guarding the entrance—from what, though? And now I think they are just trying to keep their hive warm. Yesterday—Saturday—and today are warmer and the bees are back to calmly flying in, out, and all about.

Spring Cleaning

I am always anxious and nervous when returning to the vegetable garden and exploring what the garden has done by itself in my absence. A lot, is often the answer. Now, after some spring rains, weeds, flowers, and vegetables are thriving as they compete for the sunshine and good soil. All the poppies are flowering. The large mauve Sommiferum Orientale, the sturdy Papaver rhoeas Shirley poppy with its delicate yellow, orange, and red flowers, and the single red Flanders Field poppy are in bloom. For a brief few days their mauve, orange, and red flower heads will mingle and take shelter, while the calendula push through to complete its yellow-to-orange brilliance alongside the California poppies. The borage emerges freshly invigorated from its dormancy. It has shot up and its opening flowers are welcoming the bees. The first spring flowers give early nectar to the bees and, as spring turns to summer, the little Blue Star flowers dip into our Pimm's cups' evening cocktails or decorate soft French cheeses and glisten in icing on birthday cakes. The leeks keep rising from the soil, small but strong; as always, some get away from the ongoing harvest and reseed themselves. They are as light and delicate, in a different way, as the wild French garlic that blooms in clumps of its own choosing, and is as prolific as any weed. An artichoke is emerging. So are the raspberry canes, all falling out of their wire holding pens, pushing shoots out in the exuberance of spring. There is baby asparagus, and maybe, if I am lucky, some chard and kale. It is as if they are all waving hello, welcoming me back and beckoning me to bend down and sift my hands through their dew-laden foliage. I slip my fingers and trowel into the soil, breathing softly, and am at peace for these precious moments of time.

When the grass has been weed-whacked down around the farmhouse, it immediately helps the ground dry out, and I feel as if the farm could possibly come under control and that I can choose in which direction to work. This is also the time, after pruning and during bud and blossom, that I can see what is dead. Walter TY has noted three trees on the back driveway that have not leafed out. We will take them out and then the magnificent old oak tree behind the fence to Star Route Farms will rise even more proudly. There are two young California oaks along the Franklin fence line, as well as the Churchillian English oak from Howard Dillon on the front bank by the roadside. The California oaks are planted by the scrub jays, and it is always fun to find the baby trees sprouting when the jays forget the larder in which they stashed their acorns.

There are five does out in the field, and one bobcat so far. The birds are pairing up and nesting. The sparrows are taking over the birdhouse that I had hoped would be for bluebirds. The bluebirds, are calling now, one from the telephone wire and the other from the shrubbery by the Franklin fence. There are blackbirds, chickadees, and phoebes, though I can't name as many birds as I should be able to by now. It is time to return to Keith Hansen's books so I can learn who has come to visit.

Yesterday was the first sighting of goldfinches on the farm, turning into their spring / summer plumage. They were darting across the backyard, dipping and flying over the fence for more discussion, dating, and mating in the Redwood grove. Their plumage turns just as the thistles are coming into bud. It is a synchronistic dance between the goldfinches and the thistles that both enjoy.

At least eight pairs of barn swallows have arrived at the farm and are busy beginning their nest-building on the outside of the barn that faces the front driveway. As in England, they usually arrive promptly on April 1. But this year, they are six weeks late. They showed up last evening, after teatime, swooping low and arriving in a flurry and a fuss, almost like refugees fleeing some danger. There is an urgency about their arrival. They have immediately started to bring in mud and build nests, flying up and out in a hurry: "We must catch up."

This morning, May 23, they are at it again; hurry, hurry. A little brown peeper bird is perched on the barn roof above the wisteria.

"What on Earth is going on? Why all this fuss?" she seems to be saying as her head turns this way and that.

I showed the busy builders to Chuck Oakander yesterday evening, who said Keith had found people hosing off nests from their house on Wharf Road.

"Why live here, then, if you can't engage and let nature live with you?"

Keith could not dissuade them from the destruction. My shed solution is the cardboard box, guano catcher, on the floor. We have also tacked up a small board, a poop-catcher under a beam, where some little swallow likes to build a nest by our back door rather than in the barn.

Chuck's tree crew returned and cut the birch tree back very abruptly, and it now looks like it got a flat-top teenage haircut. The arm branches are still very long, stretching out sideways as if backing away up against the fence line, with a guilty secret that adds to the teenage effect. They are just reaching out as if to gently hold hands with their first crush—the Cécile Brünner rose that guards the gate between the Franklin and Blackberry farms. The pink rose blooms are not shy, and readily entwine to glisten and shine with the emerald-green birch leaves, dipping down against the white bark of the 39-cent Safeway special bought in 1975.

An eggshell has been carried from the nest and dropped outside the barn. It is large and pale blue, and signals the first hatching, but of whose nest? Is this a starling, a red-winged blackbird, or a robin? The starlings are always the first to get busy building their nests, but where? One is always in the house chimney. Someone closed the shed door last evening when they were carefully putting everything away and the little mother swallow was shut out. She flew back in when I went to get my bike, and I hope she and her eggs will be all right. There was a good rain over the weekend and now this week is to be hot—perfect growing weather, except that I am not ready.

The pathways in the vegetable garden are all cleaned and layered with wood chips. One-and-a-half beds are weeded and clean and the other three beds still knee high in weeds. I've begun a small garden in the greenhouse. Maybe that and a couple of vegetable beds is all I get to work this year. I put in some nursery starts, the ones that beginning and (now me) old gardeners use. There are four tomato plants, three peppers, two hills of squash, and some basil. It seems manageable. I will use up the seeds I have and not buy any more this year. The scarlet runner green beans are in and the air is cool. The quail have not eaten the beans—yet. I planted the herbs I thought I had planted before, and some baby pumpkins. There are young apple trees, looking like ever-hopeful puppies, which are not yet planted. If I can get those things done, the farm will be caught up. It feels good to at least have made some progress. The soil is soft and, as always, I cannot help but take my gloves off and slip my fingers into its warmth. The bees seem to dance back and forth with the rhythm of Morris dancers, between the blue borage and the bright yellow and orange calendula flowers.

The sorrel starts that Creta gave me are doing well. They are already strong enough to split up to replant and share with others today. Edible French sorrel, Rumex scutatus, is a tough old perennial with a very long taproot. It is good to move it when the ground has begun to soften and the root can head straight down. In the wild, both here and in England, its big bully cousin dock, Rumex obtusifolius, can almost always be found growing next to stinging nettles. As children playing in the fields, when (not if) we got stung by the nettles, we knew to look for the big dock leaves growing close by. We would pull a leaf, spit, spit, spit on it, and quickly rub the spit-infused dock leaves on the bubbling blisters that rose immediately from the nettles. By the time we returned home, the blisters would already be fading, and gone by bedtime.

Today I meet with Allison, a lady from the old Point Reyes Bird Observatory, now newly named Point Blue Conservation Science, with its headquarters in Petaluma. How will they continue to have their presence felt here while reaching out to greener, monied pastures? Having their headquarters in Petaluma will not only enlarge what they want, but change from no longer being on Route One across the lagoon. The odor and aura of geography is hardly perceptible—a whiff of swamp, moist soil, an understanding of reed and weed—which is different from the dry air and harsh shrub in the Marin headlands. What will the wetlands in Petaluma bring them?

Mickey spent the last two days ploughing, seeding, and laying down plastic hoses in a section of the front field for the next cabbage family: cauliflower, broccoli, and kale. They seem to follow the lettuces in his planned crop rotation.

"Then no more brassicas in this field for a year," he says. "Maybe I can have a good spring, even if it is a bad summer." Mickey keeps smiling, even as I nudge him to make use of the back driveways for his tractor so the clumps of mud are not spat out from the tractor-tread wheels onto the front parking area, though they remind me of home and speak of serious farming.

Warren and Mickey disked their Star Route Farms and Gospel Flat fields within days of each other. Warren spread his with a concentrated fertilizer soon afterwards and the smell lasted at least thirty-six hours. This week, it's Mickey's turn. In and out, up and down went the muck spreader.

"I don't want this place smelling like the farm next door," I yelled and laughed over the tractor engine.

"It won't. The smell will be gone by this afternoon."

"What is it?"

"Horse and goat manure with grape dregs."

I paused and breathed it in. It was earthy, sweet, and good, and almost smelled of wine. Mickey drove away and over the next few hours, the compost mixture settled into the soil. Nestling in, soil embracing dung, which got busy unpacking microbes and sending them down, away from the light. Mickey was right; by teatime, the perfume had faded, along with the afternoon light.

Today there was pruning to do, and I finally cut back the overhang of the Winter Banana apple tree from across the fence. When did neighbor John Franklin plant that tree? The tree is not in the picture of us by the old chicken coop from 1975. Maybe John had planted it and it was still very small, hidden by the fallen cypress trees clinging and gasping for air around the fence line. Like the silver birch tree holding hands with the rose, the rough branches of the yellow Bellflower apple tree has reached across the fence, eager to gain support from the sturdy greengage plum tree branches. The plum is budding already, and although it is always first to promise us spring and give us a breathtaking mushroom of white, I always want to ask it to slow down, just a little. There was time to get back to weeding the bury patch. I must have staked at least six separate sweet-pea vine groupings, which look tough and hearty, belying the gentle mauve blossoms they will bring. Those sweet peas are all from one packet of seed I bought in the Deauville farmers market when we were there with *Return to Oz* in 1985!

Rhubarb, The Daffodil of the Vegetable Garden

Rhubarb is like a cat, choosing whom it will live with whom it will not. For some, it flat-out refuses the soil and situation on offer, but here, it thrives on old manure and fresh straw. Today, I picked seven pounds. Five-plus for Shorty, one-plus for Mo and Joe and the rest for us. Ed wants five pounds next week. Maybe Mickey another five this week and Shorty next. How long does the manure take to reach the roots? Two years, maybe. On the farm, I've dubbed rhubarb "the daffodil of the vegetable garden" and love all that it heralds.

Well, it is, isn't? The first edible harvest of spring. The red shoots emerging from the nubby brown rhizomes perched just at the soil level along the fence line by the septic mound, at the same time the yellow daffodils are waving hello from the front of the farmhouse. Rhubarb, Rheum rhaponticam, is actually a perennial vegetable. Grown and traded from China and the Asia-Pacific to Europe, it fetched a high price, once more expensive than saffron and cinnamon. Who gave us our first rhizome shoot? Did I find one buried deep in the undergrowth of Mrs. Peters's garden, or did it come from Michael and the nursery? Rhubarb is very happy with us. One plant quickly became two, two four, four eight, eight sixteen, sixteen thirty-two. And then I came to the end of the long border I had delegated as its home and I was out of manure with which to feed it. It grew bountifully, and still does. A few slugs and snails munch their way along the leaves, and while they rest in the early morning dew can easily be harvested for good chicken treats. I pluck the rhubarb's flower heads as soon as they unfurl. The ones I miss come into the house, and for a brief while look majestic in tall bouquets.

Rhubarb and custard was a staple springtime dessert for us as children and is one of the earliest comfort foods that English and European children remember. At home in the nursery, and later at school, rhubarb and custard was served more than once weekly. A heavenly, more adult version is rhubarb snow, a folded delight of whipped egg whites, sugar, and gently stewed pale pink rhubarb that was a child's transition to the adult table menu. In the days of seasons, of spring leading to summer, there would be a brief two weeks when rhubarb faded and strawberries emerged. Only then would the fruits join in a mixture of compotes with cream.

The first pale pink shoots of rhubarb are the product of forcing. In my father's garden were half a dozen huge clay forcing bell jars that produced the sweetest pale pink stalks, their yellow leaves barely unfolding in shyness at the dark. The pots were big enough for a child to hide in, if one didn't mind the dark and the creepy crawlies that might be in there. These delicate first stalks were tenderly brought to the kitchen in the weeks before their hardier brethren could emerge outdoors at the rate that springtime weather permitted. These would be the early treats of dining-room delight and served with fresh cream, not the custard of the nursery.

We don't have any big clay pots, but I've always been on the lookout for a couple. And now, with no horses at the farm, I have to be canny and use the skills of a poacher, harvesting the horse manure from Sally's Vanishing Point Ranch, on which rhubarb thrives. But we feed it whatever we can get. The rhubarb we grow is still excellent and the farm is one of the main producers of organic rhubarb in Marin county.

For the more discerning palate, I offer:

Rhubarb-Strawberry Mousse:

Serves **8** *to* **10**. *There are no leftovers.*

This recipe first appeared in *The New York Times* in an article by Olwen Woodier in 1989, I think. Sometime later, it was adapted from Mallards Restaurant at Arrowwood in Rye Brook, N.Y. When I found it again around 2010, I changed it a little, as you will too.

- 1¼ pounds rhubarb, finely diced

- 1 cup sliced strawberries

- ½ cup sugar

- 2 tablespoons kirsch

- 1 tablespoon unflavored gelatin

- 1 cup heavy cream

First, pick your rhubarb and buy the strawberries, or the other way around, depending where you live and even the season.

1. Combine the rhubarb, strawberries and sugar in a heavy 2-quart saucepan and simmer for 20 minutes, until the rhubarb is soft.

2. Pour two-thirds of the mixture into a blender with the kirsch; purée and set aside.

3. Pour 4 tablespoons cold water into a small saucepan and sprinkle the gelatin over the top. Allow to soften for 10 minutes. Heat gently until the gelatin has completely dissolved. Stir into the rhubarb purée.

4. Combine the purée with the remaining cooked rhubarb mixture.

5. Whip the heavy cream until stiff and fold into the rhubarb mixture. Chill for several hours.

Chapter 6

Water Ways

The Lake District

It's 1973 and the parking lot is almost empty on this late summer Saturday morning when we set out to explore the Palomarin Trailhead. Walter is leading my friend, Dolores, and I out on a new adventure. Delores is a dear nurse friend whom I have abandoned in Los Angeles; she has come with her son to visit, an overnight house call as nurses do, for the weekend. We pack a snack picnic, lace up sturdy little sneakers on the two four-year-old boys, and strap four-month-old baby Beatrice on my back. Arriving at the parking lot, we climb the short steps to the trailhead. The eucalyptus leaves and berries are undisturbed along the path which leads us down and then up the hill, alongside the black shale beach and past a plywood structure which is not yet a hut but still the beginning of the Point Reyes Bird Observatory. The trail climbs and falls as it turns inward away from the coastline for two to three miles until it comes alongside the scrapped and flattened scarping where the Lake Ranch used to stand. The farmhouse lumber has already disappeared, reclaimed and recycled into other farmhouses that are now being rejuvenated by this wave of immigration in West

Marin. On the other side of the trail, crumbling in a hollow and overgrown by vines, are the old polo stalls long ago repurposed to cowsheds. The water hole for the dairy herd lies behind the farmhouse slab. It is tranquil, with just a few mallard ducks gliding slowly through the weeds and lily pads, leaving a lazy trail of their own in the hot summer sun.

It is not far now; we walk down the willow-arched and shrub-guarded path through which the first glimmer of Bass Lake lies glistening and waiting. Memory is as clear as the lake water from those fifty years ago. There would have been one or two familial groups resting between the pines and the lake, though then, the trails led further, onto Crystal and Pelican lakes. But this was our first baptism into the lake district as it was then. We took the boys down to the water to splash, swim, and play, carrying the strapped baby along with us. The lake was clear, clean, and refreshing.

Over the years, striding into the wilderness and even just hiking to Bass Lake became a loose ritual marking family leavings and returnings. After a film came to a final end (for often, there were many "I'm finished" moments), like all artists, Walter would be exhausted, licking the wounds of creation and needing some deep rest before emerging for the family. Then, maybe on a quiet midweek day, when the children were at school, we would find ourselves on that trail again, hiking in a stillness of absorption to the lake. As we shed clothes to cover a picnic and left them under a tree, the water would call us and we would enter. Laughter before swimming the lake's length to renew our bond, sliding in and out of each other and the water, then to rest awhile before returning to the shore and beginning our life once more.

It was with others who knew the park before me that Babe and I could explore the hills, the forests, and the lakes beyond. The trails rising and falling through this end of the park were open and clear for adventure, access, and safety. The hiding of our humanity behind the smell of equine sweat gave us views into worlds that would otherwise be hidden from the clatter and chatter of hikers and, later, mountain bikers. The hours in the forest were silent but for the sound of soft hoofbeats rhythmically falling on sand and pine. Or hard, as a gallop called both Babe and me to the sheer joy of coming down a ridge trail and leaping into the depth of Crystal Lake to cool before a loose-reined, gentle ride home.

The lakes sing different siren songs for different people. For some, it is the place for gatherings with families and friends; for others, boys' own adventures with the whisper of the oceans on the other side of the forest; for still others, the cliff-edge view of sea life coming to the beach in secret, to pup or to rest awhile. Through the years, the park economy and budget have changed, and much of the park has been left to return to forest. Trails and fallen timbers are not cleared, and there is no place for the young men and women who once did such work to learn forest skills or deepen their love of the wilderness. The park is left to the wildlife, both the hunter and the hunted in the ebb and flow that bring beauty, flood, and fire with the ever-changing seasons.

Water Babe

For the year we were in London, while Walter edited *Julia* (1976-77), the farm rested in the hands of a family who had returned from wilderness living in Alaska. Fred Meader, his wife Elaine, and their boys were determined to record their life—on film.

On my return, I reclaimed our home as best I could. Some sort of schedule reassembled itself while Walter stayed in London for a further six weeks, finishing up post-production on the film. On his return we managed a break, taking a trip to Reno, where we learned from the hotel receptionist, "Elvis is dead." It was one of those remember-where-you-were-when moments. Returning from that somber trip—having lost a token amount of dollars—Walter dove into and onto the editorial team on *Apocalypse Now*. And was gone.

It must have been a Saturday in June when, after a five-hour-long screening of *Apocalypse Now* in the city, I excused myself and drove home with a headache from hell. How was I going to say, "There is so much work to do"? Turning into the farm driveway, I squashed the car brake down hard and bolted into the house, putting the kitchen kettle on before rushing up and down stairs, changing into jeans and hacking jacket as I went. Mug of tea in hand, I hurried out to the barn and, after bringing Babe in, began to brush her down. Just a short ride would help the headache and clear the rising trepidation for the months of total immersion into the work ahead that the almost daylong screening had evoked.

As I pulled the saddle down from the rack in the tack room, Babe pricked up her ears. There was a commotion going on along the back driveway. Was it rust or a deeper brown, the '60s-looking American car that slammed into the side of the hill? Now, two police cars were parked behind it. Their sirens were wailing, the doors swung open, and there was shouting. The sheriffs' warnings were returned by loud taunts and manic laughter. The shouts were getting louder, very like the film I had just left, and not taking the headache away. Peeking out the back of the barn, I could see two of West Marin's finest, hands on guns, struggling to run up the hill, chasing a jeans-clad, wild-haired man who would run, turn, and yell with laughter back to the khaki-clad sheriffs. He was fast outstripping them as he climbed the steep hill. The mindset produced after five-plus hours of *Apocalypse Now* was still a fog, but in less than a minute, Babe was saddled with the girth pulled tight and her bridle in place. I was still mounting as we swung out of the barn and into a canter along the back driveway and up the hill. The man was already on the flat field behind that house when we reached him. In a moment, he would be able to slip through the wire fence and be gone onto the ranch lands beyond. As I turned Babe toward him, she immediately picked up her pace, marking him, and moved in with a swift change of leg at each stride. He turned and twisted ahead, but she closed the ground between us. I dropped the reins and reached down across Babe's withers and over him. Babe brought him to a halt with her shoulder as I wound his hair around my hand. This was John K., well known by the community and beyond, but who had this day gone way beyond the town's tolerance level. There had been a knife and other disturbances of the peace. It took a lot for Smiley's bar to call the police to town, but John had, on this instance, become more than a menace and it was time for help.

"Don't hurt my hair." He grinned up at me and I may have grinned back at him. Babe slowed and knew to walk us at his pace as we led him down to the not-quite-as-young-as-they-were sheriffs, who were still only halfway up the hill. Handover completed, Babe and I continued slowly down the rest of the steep hill. Taking care of John had somehow begun to bring a calm to the afternoon. We just didn't usually begin a ride with a gallop up the hill. Dave Mitchell, the then-publisher of the The *Point Reyes Light*, no longer remembered my name, but there was a story—*a mounted mother of four*—and through the years to follow we would smile when we passed in the street .

★ ★ ★

There is the slightest breeze as Babe and I slip through the small gate leading into the Star Route Farms. With a loose rein, we walk along the path between the fields of vegetables and into the eucalyptus trees that bring us shade. We cross the swinging wooden bridge over Pine Gulch Creek to where, half hidden, the trail slips through the trees coming from beyond Paradise Valley and travels onward under the road to the lagoon. Entering the shallow stream-crossing, Babe stands in the moving water, cooling her legs. She paws at the water, drops her head to drink, and paws again. But behind us in this stream bed, just before the gravel rises, there is movement, stronger than the gentle ripple of the stream. A salmon is weaving sideways, trying to make her way into the lagoon. But she is stuck by the gravel. Babe's splashing about is not helping. Dismounting and slipping the reins through my arm, I bend down, cupping my hands in the water. She, for she is a she, is slippery and big. Eventually, and only because she is single-minded about where she is going, I can get both hands under her belly and lift her. I am breathless, holding the cool, silver-blue body in my hands, and I linger, knowing this is another moment when memories are made. But Babe is pulling at the reins, trying to move to where the stream is deeper, and so I move to the other side of the gravel rise. Babe drops her head back into the clear water and I bend down again, still holding the salmon. As my hands dip back into the cool water, the fish gives a twisting shudder, not quite a leap, but a push from my hands back into the stream. Suddenly, it is over. Babe continues to drink, and I slosh about and lead her to the other bank. My boots are soaked and they squish as we climb up through the high bramble hedges to the open field covered in more of Warren Weber's Star Route Farms vegetables. Babe stands as I mount, and we make our way slowly back to the road and past the school on our way home.

★ ★ ★

Babe's love of the water became a fact to know about Blackberry Farm. Maybe Carroll Ballard took it on board while he, Walter, and Gill Dennis were often at the farm, writing the screenplay for *The Black Stallion*; Carroll remembered Babe after they returned to the Bay Area for post-production. Was it Carroll or Bob Dalva who mentioned Babe at discussions with Alan Splet, for the sound effects needed to go along with the various Arab stallion's gallops on the beaches of Sardinia?

So Alan Splet and Ann Kroeber came to the farm. Between Alan and Walter, they fitted Babe with two microphones, one taped to her bridle and hanging just under her snorting nostrils, the other to the saddle girth under her belly. As the oldest child and most experienced rider, riding Babe for Alan was Carrie's project. Babe and Carrie jumped barrels and galloped past Ann and Alan again and again before it was time to head to the stream for more serious splashing. Carrying their tape recorders, Alan and Ann also brought four cement blocks to place in the water. Dutifully, Babe splashed the water hitting the blocks time and again pawing her way onto the Nagra tape recorder.

The blocks survived the onslaught of pounding and are still just holding years later as stepping stones alongside the barn. Carrie and Babe led Ann and Alan down to the beach for the rest of the afternoon. Babe jumped back and forth, in and out of the water, over wavelets as she loved to do. Dusk was falling as they returned. Carrie took care of Babe while Alan and Ann came into the kitchen to unravel and pack up their equipment. Maybe the fire was lit, flickering through the stovetop and giving warmth to the kitchen. Alan and Ann were both wet and cold, so I offered them each a glass of sherry. They were too polite to refuse, and I like to imagine that the warmth of the kitchen and the sherry, the quality of the sound effects they had gathered, and the long drive home helped them become closer.

★ ★ ★

Babe was happily handed from one daughter to another. While Carrie would look neat and trim riding this homely little mare in Pony Club and small shows, Babe took Connie into her high school rebellion. No more Pony Club for Connie! It was to be high school rodeo, and Babe changed saddles each weekend, enjoying each and every adventure. But Babe was not so tolerant of young boys and, looking back over the years now, I wonder if when she lived in Novato, maybe after her colt was born, some schoolboys had tormented her in some way. There was an incident one dark night during a late feeding, when she lunged and made contact with Walter TY's ear. Followed probably with stitches, certainly a big bandage, some hot chocolate, and more than a deep dose of parental guilt.

Babe gave us two more mares, Babe's New Penny and Ozma. Both stayed a while before going on to good homes. Even after the children had graduated, grown, and left home, Babe stayed with us, despite her crooked teeth and special chopped alfalfa. She was content as the springtime grass brought her a glossy coat and rounded belly; she enjoyed the sweetness of doing nothing but letting the sun shine on her back. Lying in the pasture was a smiling delight for her but, as the years passed, getting up, as it does for all of us, became more difficult. Though the last of her horseshoes had been long pulled and hung in the tack room, she still needed her hooves trimmed. Maurice Fitzpatrick was a whippet-thin, retired Irish farrier who drove his faded red Toyota truck down from Santa Rosa to the farm every six weeks. Unpacking his tools in the barn, he set to work with his ancient skill and understanding of old friends. With a mug of strong tea and biscuits on a tray by his side in the barn, Maurice and I would while away a morning, talking of old homes and old ways. He managed Ludi, my big Irish gelding and retired little Pony-Boy with ease. But soon, horse pal Jillie had to come and help me hold Babe upright and steady as he trimmed her feet. After months of this three-person struggle, when Maurice finished up her last hoof, he straightened up and looked directly at me. His eyes told me it was time. Babe never left the farm. The immediate release that came from her body as she slipped to the ground was all I needed to learn that my sadness was my own. Eventually, she rested in the back field where she remains, surrounded by all our herd.

The Willow Woods

Driving around the lagoon from Stinson Beach to Bolinas in the early 1970s, your eyes did not focus on any willows beyond the lagoon, but instead your gaze was drawn to the dark, glistening eucalyptus trees swaying on Horseshoe Hill. Across the water was marshland, where the Tacherra family ofttimes grazed their herd of black-and-white Holstein cattle. It was a scruffy pasture with a few willow trees that acted as shade and were held in check by the cows tramping and chewing as they saw fit. Jess Tacherra and his sons were the last of the ranchers to use that land when it still belonged to the Pepper family.

In the 1970s or '80s, while most of us were too busy raising children to see far into the future, along came one of those convergences between local government and environmentalists that refashioned the land around the Pepper farm into a field station for Point Blue Conservation Science while still keeping the very important Field Station in Bolinas. But the cattle had to go and when they left, the willow trees dug in deep. Without the cattle grazing, the Willow Woods took off. Quickly, the rough scrub slipped into the brackish lagoon, adding its own root system to knot and bind the mud. The woods have become a wilderness habitat for all creatures and the tracks through them, if not covered in bird catching and counting netting, are pathways to a magical fairyland of make-believe. They carry the seeds for childhood imaginings and the gift of freedom. The trees have grown to shade the bridge that crosses the creek's exit where it slides into the lagoon, and where, if you were six years old, you could be happy playing hours of "Pooh Sticks" or catching the ugliest of bullhead fish.

The ebb and flow of tidal water kept the trees in check for a few years but as the water's acidity changes, so does soil, and as soil changes, so does habitat. Brambles and blackberries leapt at the chance to bask in that sunshine and lay their tendrils before the trees. Creatures come—mice, rats, birds, and deer are the ones we see if we stay still and quiet enough in the dawn and dusk hours. Coming to the edge of the brackish water, the willows have paused, held in check by Don Murch's vigorous biannual mowing of pathways through the trees on his farm. Those left alongside the mowed path pause and quiver, watchful of his blade but, for now, a good barrier of roots keeps the salt water busy tussling with the encroaching trees. The willows will wait for their opportunity; when the salt and acidity of the soil change again, then they can creep forward once more.

The willows stretch out on both banks of the creek. This is where Pine Gulch Creek meets the lagoon. No longer with a splash or a roar, except in severe storms, the creek enters this body of water gently flowing, sliding, its pace and mood changing with the seasons' sun, fog, and storms. These few years are a small moment. How many will it be—five, ten, twenty more—while the lagoon, the creek, and the willows decide how to settle?

There will come a year when Don will not mow the large swatch of grassland between the two groves. And one year Don's son, Mickey, will be too busy to take on that chore. That may be the moment when the willow trees and the brackish water join and begin their march on the lagoon in earnest.

Chapter 7

Blackberry Farm: Harvests

Butterflies

Spring comes, bringing Easter within its season. We returned to the farm from the most glorious of days and Easter parties in Napa, when spring has exploded. This gathering of film folk has been an Easter tradition since we moved up from Southern California. There is a core cast of characters, similar in its fashion to the old gatherings at the Rod and Boat Club, and we welcome the chance to catch up with each other. Different productions bring guests from the casts and crews and their families. This is a family time, and we relish the heralding of these spring beginnings. The orange blossom and dogwood were in bloom, bending over and shading the fading bluebells.

The Easter weekends, when Carrie and Connie bring their Los Angeles families to visit, make for precious days together in each other's company. It is a relaxed family time, made sweeter by the granddaughters enjoying their Easter egg hunts in the long grass that has still to be cut. The buttercups and purple vetches wave cheeky hellos to the girls, teasing them with their bright yellow and purple blossoms, bobbing in the long grass while the last of the daffodil blooms bow their heads in farewell.

It was probably a Saturday morning, with the sun shining, still a tiny nip in the air, and the menfolk gathered around the kitchen table, that our eldest, Carrie, and I look at each other.

"A walk?"

"Yes."

And we hurry, scrambling to get our shoes on and out of the door before more coffee is called for or the dishes begin to overflow from the sink. Neither of us are robust hikers, and we drive to the Arroyo Hondo trailhead and park.

The trail is sheltered and truck-broad. Streams sparkle from higher, hidden springs to run seemingly with purpose down one side of the hill, over or under the trail, and dive into the deep gully on the other side. Bay, oak, and redwood trees hold the madrone, honeysuckle, and brambles along the banks. Wildflowers, columbine, and forget-me-nots that we try to tame in our gardens are happy in their hamlets beside the trail. Mosses are sprouting their hairy-tip gametophytes stems like antennae, while the mushrooms drop their spores down as they both cling to and embrace the trees. The trail is damp and, in parts, waterlogged. We are mindful of the late-night banana slugs that are still making their way out of the sun and home to a wet and shady pile of leaves.

Looking around as we walk, we can see this year's damage. The trees whose roots have lost their hold on the ever-changing bankside now lie broken and fallen. Most have been cut away as the utility trucks still need to get through to check the small reservoir ahead.

It is just a mile and a half to the trail's end, or where it ends now. There were years gone by, not that long ago, when we could ride through the forest, up or down the ridge, slipping into and around hidden lakes, the horses careful and knowing of the trails kept open by the deer. The forest is a magical place, but each year, it closed its gates a little more. For a while, we could still make our way through the fallen trees, but then Pan and his family finally had enough of our ramblings. Fearing we had come too close in hunting the forest's secrets, a strong winter storm felled the final barrier. Steadily, the shrubs and plants closed back over the fallen trees.

Carrie and I walked on, talking of this and that. She enjoyed telling of her world, and I enjoyed listening. That is how it is; a daughter grows in assurance and strength, sharing her own decisions and just returning to check in, harvesting approval as well as caution.

Quite suddenly, turning one corner into bright sunlight, we were met by a silent burst of small, blue butterflies, spring azure from the Lycaenidae family, who had just this hour emerged from their chrysalises. These were males, puddling and hanging out at the water hole as chaps do, looking for the ladies while getting a drink and some nosh from the mud and nearby flowers. Within hours of the poor girls emerging, the males grab and have their way with them. The next day, her tiny body changing once again, poor love, she lays her eggs on the nearby plants and then dies.

No counting of how many there were. We enjoyed the caress of their soft wings as they rose from drinking in the puddle and supping from the blue forget-me-nots. We walked on up to the small ponds and sat by the old waterwheels for a while. The water is clear here, and trout have been known to rest under the banks on the far side. How they get there and where they go is a journey I have not followed.

Resting on the soft moss and enjoying the cool air rising from the pool, we laughed at how and when I had first learned about this little spot. It would have been just about the time that Carrie and Connie were settling in to live with us, and today is a time to share and weave more childhood memories together. The pool was a Mother's Day gift from a very young Walter. At six years old, he had made my breakfast and brought it up to me in bed. As the tray sat precariously on my lap, he announced I should get dressed. He was taking me fishing. While I ate breakfast, he loaded the truck with all that we would need. Once out of the driveway, he guided me along the road to the trailhead. We walked, mostly in silence, as he purposefully led the way to this spot. We fished. And it was good. And we had a snack (I had been told to bring a snack) and came home. It was a perfect morning in every way. And now, here was another perfect memory, made with Carrie.

Returning along the path, we came back to the puddle. Now, there were just a few unlucky fellow butterflies hovering around the mud who would soon die a virgin's death. We walked on and returned home. The men were still talking at the table and some dishes had been washed, yet there was more food to prepare.

And then Carrie and Connie and their Los Angeles families are gone. They come for holiday moments, families migrating in, landing like butterflies, resting, sipping nectar from the home farm, and leaving again. It happens more and more, yet I am still not taking in what is going on. The farm remains the harbor, and I am anchored within the farm, though the waters can be choppy at times. I return to the land, the kitchen, the laundry, and my bistro table.

Taking Flight

Maybe even just that morning, it could have caught my mother's eye in the bookshop window and on impulse, she went in. Back at home, she wrapped Jane Pilgrim's *The Adventures of Walter the Duck at Blackberry Farm* into a package she was putting together to give to the vicar's daughter. Just as I had eight years earlier, Rachael was leaving her village. The first stop of her new life adventures was to San Francisco, staying safely (!) with us on the houseboats. Rachael and her parents— the vicar and his wife—must have come for a teatime visit, and my mother, as was her wont, didn't miss an opportunity to say, "Can you take these with you?" and deftly slip Rachael a squidgy bundle to put into her already overstuffed suitcase. With the fresh purchase of the farm, the book echoing the father-and-son family names, and with the overwhelming blackberry vines, it was only natural that Peters Dairy became Blackberry Farm. And like Jame Pilgrim's imagined Blackberry Farm, ours was soon busy with children, creatures great and small, and farm life. We arrived with two children, one horse, a dog, and two cats. Through the years, they all multiplied. When Carrie and Connie came to live with us, two children became four; and one horse, Babe, became several ponies, a dog or two, and several cats. The farmhouse filled to overflowing as friends added to family and tables expanded as needed. Even the farm grew when our original four-plus acres eventually became seven.

Children and animals came in equal measure until the children grew up and away, the horses lay buried in the fields, with the smaller creatures all rolling over into the bury patch garden bed where they were remembered and resurrected in the flowers that grew over them. While there are still bees, pears, rhubarb, sheep, and more chickens, the ebb and flow of farm life now takes on a different rhythm. The small apple orchard that I began hangs on, producing exquisite apples for all purposes even as the gophers take their tithe.

Our families all return to the farm regularly. But when Walter said softly but clearly, "All things being equal, I would be very happy living with you in London," I and the universe heard him. He began to work with Taghi Amirani on *Coup 53* in 2015, roaming the city streets of his choosing, while the farm rested in the chambers of my heart.

Soft Landing at an Ace Café

To drive up the old Roman road, the A30, to London's Heathrow Airport was a summer Saturday-night thing to do in the early '60s. We would race the two red sports cars, Jack's Austin-Healy Sprite and Dennis's Standard Triumph TR2, to the Ace Café, where we joined the motorcycle riders who grudgingly allowed us room to park the cars. We would have a drink—bitter lemon for Susette and me—and sit for a while outside under the bright café lights, looking up at the planes flying above us in the night sky to who knew where. Then, our curiosity barely satisfied with glimpsing unknown dreams yet not ready to take off and fly away, we would turn back, facing the road home to the countryside. It was on one of those A30 returns, coming out of Camberley and crossing the old but still used Blackbushe Airport, that I pushed down hard with my kitten-heeled shoe and topped my first 100 mph in the TR2, the road flashing past in a gap in the floor underneath the clutch pedal as the two cars, now driven by the girls, raced home. In the end, I was the only one of us to fly from our small corner of Hampshire and eventually, with my budding wings quivering, board a plane rising high over the Ace Café.

★ ★ ★

"You're spending a lot of money on this horse stuff." So muttered a sleepy husband in 1977 in London.

"Well, it's not my fault if you are not extravagant. Go out and buy something," was the flip response before we both fell asleep. A week later, the conversation continued again in the dark.

"I've found something."

"That's wonderful. What is it?"

"A desk. It's very expensive."

"How much?"

"£125. And it's very big. Too big to go in the house."

"That's not expensive. And it can go above."

"Above what?"

"The barn."

"It's a plot." And with that tactical agreement, we went back to sleep.

It wasn't really a plot but more like a progression, taking the moment and momentum when we could move forward. On returning to the farm from *Julia's* completion in London, we managed a short break before Walter quickly moved into the editing team on *Apocalypse Now*. Always, after being away, there is the reclaiming, making the house your home again.

That year spent in London had been a wonderful time for gathering our four children into a family. Away from their old friends, they turned to each other, becoming siblings while tentatively making new friends at their separate schools. But the British school system is very different from anything they had had before. Carrie and Connie went to Acland Burghley, the Tufnell Park Comprehensive. Walking through the entry hall on the first day of school, there was a sign on the notice board: *Wanted for Murder*. I wondered about that. After the first chaperoned trip through the underground system, changing northern lines at Camden Town, they happily went off in their black-and-gray uniforms and satchels. Eight-year-old Walter TY walked to All Saints, an old church school that had just become a state-run school in Hampstead, and I took three-year-old Beatrice on the bus to a nursery school off Finchley Road in Swiss Cottage. At the end of each day, I gathered them all back together and we had a family teatime moment. In that one year, a gentle rhythm imposed itself on the family, from Walter's English work hours being more regulated to the school days that brought a new kind of peace to our lives. The adventures were manageable and fun. We drove to the countryside to visit with my mother and for the children to get an undercoat of understanding and memory of their mother's childhood. There were Sunday lunches with friends and family and a couple of wild winter weekends spent driving Carroll Ballard and Tom Sternberg to Arab horse-breeding farms, looking for potential stallions for *The Black Stallion.*

But now we were back from our migration and an American rush overtook us, even on the farm. On any level of returning, there is always laundry. With a traveling family of six and a quick household turnaround, there were now mountains of it taking up the entire laundry room, and I hated it. The laundry was eventually tamed, brought into a manageable rhythm, along with all the household chores that go to keep a home functioning in a measure of comfort. Six weeks later, Walter returned from London to the farm, and for a brief moment he and I took off, driving up to Reno.

Upon returning from the mini-getaway, Walter began his first day on *Apocalypse Now.*

I took a deep breath and also began. It had been John Pullen's small racing barn in Church Crookham that allowed me to see it. A small stable with just six stalls, three and three facing each other. If that design was modified to allow a truck and trailer to drive through a center aisle, I would not have to keep backing and turning a big rig in the driveway. A barn to replace the existing barn, to fit in with the farm style, and, as importantly, to pass through the permit process. It was Jill's husband, architect Ron Young from the houseboats, who understood and brought the barn from dream to reality.

The Hay Loft "above" was where the desk landed for many years and, to this day, the Looking Glass Films company office still holds a corner of that space. But before that, when it was only a plywood floor with plumbing, it became another Ace Café, where friends in migration could land, pause to refresh for the months they needed before moving forward with their lives.

★ ★ ★

In the springtime, the view from the farm kitchen window to the front driveway looks like another Ace Café of its own. Year-round resident birds now dip and glide in with a similar swagger to the regular bikers as they emerge from the woodlands to check out "what's happening." They perch on the telephone and electrical wires, the pasture fence lines, the tops of cars, and the barn roof. They are busy, eyeing each other and the arrival of the migrating swallows. Some swallows reach the barn early enough to rest and catch up with each other on the high wires. The farm driveway is busy for days as the migrating birds take time for their soft landing and to reacquaint themselves with those full-time residents who stay all year long. March 25 is truly a date marked by their arrival. The sparrows and finches fly off the wires in a huff. Bluebirds skid and slide onto the roofs of our dusty cars, pointing out this and that real estate deal. Soon it is time to get busy with each coupling, joining with their old or a new partner for this spring season to stake out a space in and around the barn where the pecking order becomes apparent—the early birds, the young birds, the first-time builders, the returnees, and the bullies. Now the birds all mix: the barn swallows, the sparrows, the bluebirds, and the phoebes circling and claiming their places in the rafters, under the eaves, along the beams, and even in the stall mangers. Behind the barn, in the redwood grove, the male hummingbirds soar and dive, like the ace motorbike riders on the A30, flashing colors and prowess to entice the ladies to join them high above the redwood fronds. A

Bullock's oriole takes the blue nylon hay-baling twine to weave into a hanging nest in a poplar tree. In front of the barn, amidst the roses and honeysuckle, another female hummingbird sets up home. More sparrows push their way into the roses while the finches fly higher and are secretive in the trees and the thick hedges. Once again, it is the girls who do the building, setting up house, though the males may help them carry materials to the site she has selected.

Year after year, the red-winged blackbird families bury themselves in the grasses and reeds beside the pond and across the road. The males call, display, and guard, perched on the bull rushes and wild white rose beside gate and pond. The starlings, slobs that they are, often nest in the fireplace chimneys. Several times throughout the summer, a fledgling falls down the chimney and ends up in the stove. We wake to the sounds of panic as a young bird scrambles and pushes against this dark sooty prison. There is a procedure to follow: open the front door and raise the front windows, and only then open the stove door. Sometimes it takes a minute or two for them to realize they are free before they fly, usually straight out of the open window or door. We always hope they explain the situation to the rest of the brood. But they never seem to, and soon enough, someone else falls—*plop!*—down the chimney. From time to time, our border terrier, Hana, would have her brother, Brodie, come to visit while his person, Eileen Brown, returned to Scotland to be with her parents. Brodie never landed softly but bounced into the farm, jumping and smiling and drooling with happiness. It was easy to tell that Brodie loved these visits. There were walks, there was a smaller sister terrier to boss, and there was the stove. As evening came, the dogs moved from the back of the sofa, a good window-watching perch, to lie on the floor beside the stove. The dogs curled up close together, the warmth from the stove infusing their dreams, making the day's run or catch longer and bigger than any fisherman's tale. Sometimes, if the season was right, the stove would produce a morning treat, with a starling flying directly into Brodie's mouth. Delight and surprise were followed by pain and serious hurt feelings if we, and the starling, were lucky enough to rescue it.

More than a pair, and thus a wake, of mourning doves have found the farm. Is it the chicken grain that has brought them? They perch on the wires, the barn, anywhere they can before deciding where to nest. I'd envisioned a dovecote, but have been strongly voted down. The doves' incessant cooing and calling can rise above the lighter chirping and overwhelm the sky.

★ ★ ★

Coming in waves, we all migrated here, each generation finding a place to settle and make the best of our gifts and lives that we could. Where is that place of "relative safely and comfort" where we can do our best work, whatever that happens to be? Sometimes friends needed a soft landing before reaching their destination. The community has always been full of such places and the farm has often been one of them.

Sally pulled in from Nicasio, driving her truck and pulling the horse trailer loaded with two horses and a cat. There was tack and feed for the horses, and not much else. The shift in balance of ranches and real estate had picked up again. Pockets were etched out of hillsides, and country homes were settling into ranches as taxes and retirement continued their encroachment on supposed security. Sally stayed on the farm for a while before, with horse pal Susie Whaley's help, finding her own nesting site and making her home and life in the community.

"You should go and spend a couple of months with Aggie in California," said horse trainer chum William Blake to Rosie Barry over a cup of tea in his Leominster farm kitchen as he and

Rosie mulled over another of life's knotty problems. And so she did and, like Sally, landed at the farm and stayed for a while. Rosie created Sam's House and, with her beloved Julio, cared for many of the seniors who wanted to live their final years close to their families in this community. There were to be more folks from the different parts of our lives all needing a pause to catch a breath before moving on. Sometimes a soft landing was all that was needed before leaving town.

A little VW rabbit coughed and spluttered to a stop in the driveway in the early hours of a July 5 morning. Creeping downstairs and out into the dark driveway, I found two young girls from the city parked safely under the purple plum tree. They had come to town for the July Fourth celebrations and made a stop at Smiley's. Now they were not at all sure they could make it back to the city.

"It's okay. Come on up into the barn. There are blankets and quilts."

"Oh, we are fine here. Are you sure?"

Quietly, we climbed up the stairs and they settled softly together on the sofa in the hayloft.

"Please don't tell Walter." And I realized they were two of the ever-eager young women who roamed the halls of American Zoetrope, doing whatever odd jobs came their way. They did not want to be seen in this evening light. By daylight, the driveway was empty once more.

The hayloft has always held a bed as well as a desk, and been a place of refuge. Like the Ace Café perched on the edge of the old A30 road to London, there is a view. For us, now, it is our destination, a place of refuge when we return home to Bolinas and gather strength for the journey ahead.

The Detritus of War

On sunny autumn mornings, the house would shudder as the backhoe rumbled along the Gospel Flats road past the farm. Rick Klaes sat tall in his seat, driving this steady workhorse with ease and confidence into town or up to the mesa. He had the delicate light touch needed from a man to drive the big rig, turning her this way and that as if in a slow swing dance until he had her bucket right where he wanted for the job at hand. Rick was a tall man, thin with the scrawny tautness of scrappy years that had left their mark in his face and body. He proudly wore his uniform of old Levi's, worn leather jacket, and an even older leather hat that looked more Australian than American and appeared molded to his head.

Backhoes fill a much-needed niche in rural communities. Mostly, there is just a steady drip-drip of jobs, one or two a week, not enough for its owner, Bill Albright, to pull away from his garage and vegetable garden where he was happiest for those semi-retirement years. Occasionally, a storm caused a rush of work, and then everyone had to wait their turn. The same back-hoe could live in a town for decades, passed from one owner to another. It is even more important than the local gas station, for there were plenty of men—and women—who knew how to hot-wire a car, change a tire, and determine which fluid was leaking out of which hose under a truck's hood. As long as Rick could drive for Bill, then Albright held onto his old machine.

What bound these two men for the years they worked together? What did Bill recognize in Rick when he had swept up on the local beach and somehow found his way to Albright's farm?

Or did he miss it, mistake the painful disease that comes from inside our genetic makeup to an exterior influence? Did

Bill see Rick's earnest efforts to make a life and try to give this guy one more chance? Bill's patch of a few acres was at the turn where the lagoon road began its journey as Gospel Flats, named for the churches that lined the road into town in the nineteenth century. St. Mary's Catholic Church still sits active at the bottom of Horseshoe Hill Road, while the Druid's Hall became tucked into Star Route Farms. The Presbyterian trundled, literally, into town and was later joined by the little Episcopalian Church of St. Aidan's. Bill Albright's small acres were a little off the beaten track, though everyone who came in and out of town had to pass by it. Every year, at least one truck will still take that corner too fast and end up in a ditch. This could have accounted for Bill holding onto his backhoe for so long.

Rick was holding on too. But the job was not enough to keep his demons and nightmares at bay. What caused the final slip with Bill and Rick? Does it matter? For it happens in all walks of life; the turmoil and terror of internal and external wars do not end when the fighting stops. Throughout history, the demons of addiction or the horrors of war do not preclude each other's presence. Separately or together they can prance and prick the mind until the membranes that hold madness at bay are stretched to breaking. Drink helps and so do drugs—for a while.

As a child in England, I watched old warriors who had returned from both World Wars. Mothers and wives minded that the children were seen and not heard as we roamed the dark corridors of the clubhouse while the men stood resolutely holding up the bar at the North Hants Golf Club. Mornings and afternoons, in all weather, they strode onto the course as if into military maneuvers, trying to calm their minds with the control of their bodies, reaching for the rugged fresh air, rough Ulex gorse shrubs, purple Calluna vulgaris heather to heal them. The brute force needed to get a ball out of that rough helped a little, but after the final putt was holed on the 18th green, their clubs put away in the shed, cleats exchanged for brogues in the gentlemen's cloakroom, then memories returned, leading them back to the 19th hole and pints of sherry and whiskey. Beer was for boys.

There were more than a few men such as Rick in our town. Mostly they lived low, cruising from one hangout to another. Occasionally, a relative was near enough to reach out a hand, an old car, a shack out back. Ofttimes it was another—a friend, close or even casual, who knew help was needed and was willing to give it.

Some still remember Scowley's as an old-fashioned breakfast-and-lunch café run by Paul and June Fontan. Situated on Wharf Road, across from Smiley's Saloon, it was a bright and cheerful place to be, one of the last of the old eateries after Tarantino's was burnt to the ground. When the 1971 oil spill happened, Randy and Helen fed the volunteers who were placing the straw barricade at the mouth of the lagoon while desperately trying to clean up the beach, the birds and each other. After Paul died, his sons Randy and Gary, with their wives, Helen and Linda, took up the apron strings, turned on the coffee, and fired up the range. As the oil-spill crisis faded from the immediacy of the town, as if pulled out with the ebb tide before being sucked into a statewide political courtroom, people who had come for the excitement of helping to clean up discovered the beauty of Bolinas and lingered. Scowley's became a hangout where young and old vets of all wars would go. There was a fluidity in the kitchen, in the cooler, and at the counter. There was a piano and music. And the bruised and broken men came, some holding onto a job, some climbing out of the abyss and terror that remained with them, and some abandoning it all. Above all, this was a place of brotherhood.

Sitting at the counter at Scowley's, the men could relax. They owned it. Boaz, Bald Eagle, Icon, and Pluto were just a few of the men who came to rest here at that time. Jobs were offered and picked up over a cup of coffee or outside on the street, leaning on the tailgate of a truck. Many were winging it below the water line of this lifeboat in town, now as worn down as its customers. But the town was changing and there was someone in the wings waiting to clean up and refresh this little corner. With the closure of Scowley's, the men were set adrift. Many wandered across the road to Smiley's for a drink or a fight, and were frequently tossed from the bar. At times, when Rick had returned from an overnight wash and brush-up in jail, I would find him standing, waiting hesitantly, by the library and community center, looking warily over at Smiley's.

"How is today, Rick?"

"I'm afraid to cross the road."

The Shop, another restaurant run by Gwen and Bud Spangler, had a quiet, understanding, and kindly table set out most nights for someone who needed Bud's clam chowder— guaranteed to calm anyone down before they went back out onto the street and into the night air. There were few places left to go; there were bushes, the street, the beach, and the little covered gate into the Episcopal church where one could sit down and drink. They were moved on from one spot to another, drinking more, fighting more, and washing less.

We never went into Scowley's. The laughter across the counters shot out of the windows as barks. The Fontans had put in billiard and ping-pong tables for the young teenagers cruising between the danger that was in the air downtown and the safety of our and other farm kitchens with girls and cookies, slipping into safer waters for rest. Teenagers of any breed learn to smell danger and respond to it according to their age and ability. In these years, young boys who knew the sounds of safety and danger responded to them, along with the village gifts of the fluidity of family. The Fontan family was a brotherhood of four: the twins Randy and Greg, known as Coon, just from the look of him; Gary, who bore kidney disease and diabetes, who died in 1985-86; and the younger brother, Chris. Donald Walker, named Boaz, a brother in service in Vietnam with the Fontans, came to Bolinas searching and finding the comradeship and universal understanding towards each other that needed no explanation. The Vietnam War was not yet in the distant past. Pain was to be relieved by any means possible. In the late 1980s, Boaz got into one fight too many and died from a head injury two weeks later. Boaz's wife Emily wanted a proper send-off for Boaz.

★ ★ ★

It is pissing with rain. Pissing—a steady stream that is a relief, yet will feel so good when it stops. But it doesn't, and Emily has arrived at the church doors. She is carrying a five-gallon plastic water jug covered in American stickers with Boaz's ashes lying in the bottom. She walks firmly up to the altar and places the jug on the white altar cloth. Emily is accompanied by Boaz's tribe. Others are now following, and soon the little Episcopal Church of St. Aidan's is full and steaming as the body warmth draws off the dampness from the wool sweaters and leather jackets the men are wearing. It is mostly men, though Janice and a few more women join them. Rick's leather cowboy hat is firmly on his head, and those wearing hats do not take them off in the church.

A gray minivan is parked at the lych-gate. Huddled in it are six Marines wearing dress uniforms, and they do not want to get wet. They are waiting until they absolutely must, before they clamber out of the van and march to the wooden church doors.

The vicar has to hold himself steady, realizing that, for today at least, the town and street people have claimed his church, and though the church is working just fine, this isn't quite how he had imagined it. The service starts. There are prayer books and hymns, someone plays the old piano, and this congregation lifts a union of rasping voices in long-remembered songs of praise. They tolerate this music and the intonations and the prayers, for they know that at some point the vicar must ask if anyone has anything to say. He is dreading it; they are longing for it. For they all have something to say.

Almost to a man, they speak of Boaz's talent in music, his courage, his good heart. But nobody speaks of their war. This takes a long time and though the vicar wants to cut them short, he doesn't dare. Finally, the service is over, and the vicar leads everyone outside where, suddenly, the sun comes out.

Now it is time, and safe, for the six Marines to get out of the damn van and march up the little path from the lych-gate to the church doors. They are carrying the United States flag and a boom box. One holds the flag up high while another puts the box down on the ground beside them and presses play. As the trumpet music comes from the boom box, the town's men surrounding Emily all now remove their hats, and with a hand on their hearts, stand to attention, holding Boaz and their secrets close to their hearts. Two Marines take the flag and fold it correctly, as they must. Then one steps forward and hands Emily the folded flag, which she proudly accepts with her head held high. The men around her watch with solemnity, some knowing that one day, this service will be done for them.

We have made coffee and brought plates of sweet treats, which serve to gently release the tension of the morning. It is a completion, the breaking of bread, the quiet sipping of hot, strong, sweet coffee together. Slowly, and then suddenly, they are all gone, disappearing into the town's jungle, carrying their pain and secrets with them.

★ ★ ★

It's the winter of 1982 and Diane Horvath has died after an exhaustive battle with cancer. Timmy and Alex are two of her six children. They are gathered together and the house needs to be cleaned for the relatives who are coming to visit. Thankfully, there was a neighborhood of friends who came to help, though it was hard to know where to start. My mother, Granny Slater, was visiting with us at the farm, and together we took the truck up to the little yellow house on the mesa. We combed through the house, stuffing every bit of laundry we could find into gray pillowcases. The back of the pickup was full and we drove downtown to the laundromat. Granny and I unloaded the truck and dumped everything on the laundromat floor before sorting: colors and whites, to bleach or not to bleach (bleach everything). We filled up a row of machines. My mother went next door to the liquor store where, understanding the need, Janet happily took our dollars, giving my mother all her quarters. Click, click, and slam the quarter slots, machines shut, and the water pours in. The skies darkened as the rain came. This storm was to rage through the winter for days at a time, such was the God's anger at the loss of a mother. By the time the washing machines were spinning the end of their cycles, the men from the streets had arrived, seeking shelter and warmth. The little room became crowded and moist with the men, my mother, and me. More dollars and quarters changed hands. As the afternoon chores called me back to the farm, I left my mother, the laundry, and the gentlemen of the street together for forty-five minutes.

The rain was falling steadily now, no longer in a rage, though the sky was getting even darker when I returned. But there was a warm glow beyond the florescent ceiling lights in the laundromat. And there was laughter. And there was my mother, with Bald Eagle, Rick, Pluto, and others, folding sheets. They could have been dancing. It was clear that when my mother had needed help, to a man, they leapt to her aide. They were helpful and gallant and proud, and, for a too-brief half hour, happy.

Chapter 8

Summary

After the spring rains, the lilies' shiny green leaves sit in clumps, covering anything and everything in their way. As suddenly as with any spring bulb, the leaves die back and disappear, returning and sinking into the soil, and the plants hide in the dark. When summer peaks, their thick stems—a palette mix of brown and pink that have been pushing up from the long-dead, lush spring leaves alongside both driveways—stretch upward silently, like a cat stalking its prey, as they reach toward the light. Until suddenly, on a bright, sunny day, they are there. Naked Ladies, Amaryllis belladonna, bursting into a flaming hot-pink abundance, clumped together (the bulbs need to be crowded to flower), and they look like a gaggle of middle school cheerleaders about to go onto a football field. They are the last of the summer bloomers in the garden. Vegetables are bursting all over their patch, and roses, lavender, and dahlias are still lingering, but there will be no more brilliant new flowers until the mauve Michaelmas daisies open their tiny aster heads for the bees in September. It is tempting to pluck the long-stemmed flowers, and all the newcomers to town do it once. But only once, for when inside the house, the strong pink blush of blooms suddenly looks brash, overdressed, and out of place. Like surly children covering their country embarrassment, they emit the most awful rotten smell, and have to be dispatched before night has fallen.

As I write, a young woman has parked her bike, unloaded her backpack, sipped from her water bottle, and now squats with her camera, taking pictures of the pink ladies who guard our gateway and the blackberries that encircle the ladies. Rising from the ground, she plucks one stem and takes the flower with her.

Lavender

It is late June before I manage to pick the first of the Grosso French lavender to sell at the farmstand. I could have, should have, started to pick a week earlier when the flower heads were just beginning to open. But I was late; trying to catch up after being away, I missed the gray buds and only caught the flowers as they darkened to their deep purple. There is already a touch of brown as the first petals die off, but only a touch. One plant gives eight bunches, which is twenty-four dollars. The plants I harvested last year produce the best flowers this year. So I learned what has been so obvious for centuries to lavender farmers in the south of France: that harvest, which doubles as pruning, keeps the plants healthy and strong for the four-plus years they can last before becoming too woody. I will keep harvesting the Grosso, the Alba, and maybe even some English. There are as many bumble as Italian bees on the lavender.

Because of the drought and my continued inability to water, I will plant more lavender in the spaces in the front border. Can I fill up the first Grosso lavender harvest of the year with sweet pastel blooms of late spring? Lavender and late-summer Michaelmas daisies that always keep the bees happy? And can I add more drought-resistant butterfly plants between the lavender and Michaelmas daisies? I was sad to mow the great yellow-and-white clover from the arena yesterday. The bees will miss that. But there are many more varieties of butterflies. What am I seeing and/or recognizing on the farm?

Western Tiger
Swallowtails
Monarchs
Cabbage White

Common Buckeye

Red Admirals

Today is a beautiful day. The Souvenir de Mme Léonie Viennot, living up to its long name, is now more than forty feet long, looped and hung over the front field fence. It is a pink hedge rose in full bloom, and the birds flitting about make the roses duck and bob in the still air. My mother loved rambling, climbing roses, and I imagine this one reaching up to her as she rests on the mountain, looking down on the farm and smiling at our successes and our failures. God bless the spirit.

We had a belated birthday party for Randy Thom with a gathering of mostly the old KPFA Pacifica Drama and Literature radio heads, and the new ones from KWMR Community Radio, with just a sprinkle of film fellows. After the film folk left, sensibly driving home before the darkness overtook them on the mountain road, the tight band that surrounded our leader, Erik Bauersfeld, lingered on. We had dragged a table out into the back where we now all sat together. The barbecue grill was still, with smoking embers dying as they drifted onto the porch. Plates of leftover snacks lay casually on the table while we absorbed the evening round of vodka and wine. We sat together, the party proper having dissolved into the night, sharing the comfort and deep friendship that this small community of radio men and women give to each other, lingering old hands from KPFA: Erik Bauersfeld, Randy Thom, Susan Stone and Jim McKee, Lyons Filmer, and me now joined by Kay Clements and John Gouldthorpe from KWMR, along with those who slipped into film to earn their keep. Walter, too, had had his early roots in radio. The summer of 1961 found him at WRVR in Riverside Church, working as a record librarian and even announcing. He followed this up in 1961 and '62, putting time in as a DJ at the Johns Hopkins college station, WJHU. The sunlight was fading as we listened to Erik weaving his stories with his musings on art and literature. The comfort of his age, his stories, and life lulled us into an evening of peace and laughter, with just enough intellectual discussion to make us think we might be being meaningful. The dishes would wait; they always do. Only when the bottles of wine and vodka were emptied was it time for this solid crew to wend their way back into their urban worlds. When everyone had gone home, I put the leftover barbecue bones out on the tin plate going into the back field. There were none left in the morning.

Another Farm Friday

Thought I had left the well water on, for twenty-four hours, yikes—it was still running. My Friday farm day was perfect with a full three hours. The middle vegetable bed was raised up with the last of the railway ties, blocking the not-fitting holes with chunks of eucalyptus logs, and then weeded.

After weed-whacking around the greenhouse, we went into the apple orchard to plant the last five young trees. Poor trees. The ground was pickaxe-hard and so were the root balls around the little trees. A break, and then, with an afternoon cup of tea in hand, I went through the adult trees, nipping and tucking. There was very little pruning to do, very few diseased leaves or dead branches. Even the trees I had marked with orange baling twine for watching, (and maybe whacking) were looking healthy. There was only one Ashmead's Kernel way back of the orchard to come down. It felt so good to have those young babies in the orchard.

Today started out sunny and warm. But now, the wind is racing around the farm and house, tormenting any area that is not sheltered. It beats away at the swallows' nests on the front of the barn. This morning, there were seven nests. This afternoon, only five. Half of one lies on the concrete, a shattering of mud. The other nest fell completely, bringing with it the hurried interweaving of grasses. Usually, the swallows are neat tenants and it is the sparrows who are the barn slobs, leaving long wisps of old hay and straw and someone's feathers drifting and falling about all over the place. These swallow nests look hurried; the swallows knew they were late and had to rush through this bit of building. But when the second nest fell, there was a speckled egg and a tiny embryo open. I swept it all up and put the mud, straw, and baby in the compost pit. Another nest is drying out.

Will the nighttime moisture enter it and keep it safe for a few more hours? Little faces peek out from the remaining nests. Not the babies yet, just the young mothers, unsure if this is really a safe neighborhood in which to bring up their families.

Mickey is busy reseeding his squash plants. He is doing battle with the gophers below and the crows above. He shows me a soft hole where a gopher is waiting for the seed, and a small baby crab brought and left by a crow as it moves onto the next course of salad! Mickey trudges along the freshly planted rows, hauling white plastic row covers to lay over the new crops. The wind tries to pull them from him, but he is still young and strong.

The row of broccoli he put in is not good. He was late with his planting here. So many mistakes to make! He sighs, but it is not so much a sigh to the world as a scolding against himself for getting it wrong. He is young enough to believe he should not make such mistakes, but this is not a mathematics quiz. Half of the broccoli is full of aphids, and the chickens will love that. The other half is tight, bright, and bitter, though it cooked up well. Just not great, which is what we have come to expect.

I can even feel the wind coming down the chimney in the dining room. But it is sunny too. Early, as I bike the road around the lagoon, I saw the Canadian geese getting big. The baby goslings are so well protected by their parents that they are hard to spot with the naked eye. Walking to the nursery and back in the late winter and early spring, we are aware of the geese pairing on Warren's wet field, but then we see nothing. Warren ploughs the field under, the geese disappear, and there are no goslings or toddlers until suddenly, now, as summer comes, there are teenagers and young-adult geese. They are still following their parents as family units, seemingly joined in lines of slightly slighter, slimmer geese, eventually breaking into teenage gaggles. How long will they stay before they fly away? Do they go back to Canada as in Canadian geese? Do Canadian geese actually go home again? Back in the house, Mitzi stays with me, making her daytime business occur around my business.

A hatch of fledgling sparrows are perched up in the birch tree. The upper, outer branches are a good place for the young sparrows to hang out, hang tight for their "Oh, my gawd, do I really have to—can I—fly from here?" moments. They are swaying and fluttering their wings, begging to be fed one more time, and they are as the parents come to them again and again, stuffing little cobweb-caught creatures into the ever-open beaks. When does that end? When the babies get too big for the nest or they separate as a family?

★ ★ ★

After cleaning up outside, I managed a midday shower before treating myself to a sit-down lunch, and Don Deane phoned.

"Bees in the rock wall."

"How many?"

"One-fifty."

"No. How big?"

"A basketball."

"I'll have lunch and then come down."

"Right, I'll go out and count them."

After lunch, I packed everything into the car and drove down. It was a small swarm, maybe half a pound at most. It took some fiddling and shifting to place the hive at the right height below the swarm, then to gently smoke and sweep the bees into it. I had to keep doing it, smoke and sweep a few times before Don and I could sit together on the wall, each of us with a mug of coffee in hand and time for a long overdue catch-up. Don is tired and ready for the next stage of his life. He is deeply relieved that Smiley's Saloon is looking to be sold. It was in about 1975 that he retired as a Marin County probation officer and loosened his ties with Carolyn Brown's Full Circle program for young boys in need of extra care and support. Don began *The Coastal Post* newspaper, balancing its weekly publication, life with his foster kids, and then Smiley's. As he clears out his saloon papers, he is also sorting out and packing up memories of the Coastal Post office, which was above the Saloon. He dreams of his campsite in the Sierra Nevada and longs to move there full time. This information is more absorbed than spoken, understood and ingested along with the coffee while we waited until almost all the bees had moved into the hive box and I took them home. It is one of those "a swarm in July is not worth a fly" swarms, but I put them in a little hive body and fed them some honey water. There is some kind of ritual, almost an unspoken mantra when you welcome new life to the farm, and you never know what will happen.

A swarm in May is worth a load of hay,
A swarm in June is worth a silver spoon,
A swarm in July is not worth a fly.

Finally, I have a moment to quietly sit outside, watching the sparrows and finches feed their second hatching of brood. It is a frantic time for the parents, trying to get the babies fledged and out of the nest before the end of summer. It is exhausting just to see them working so hard on this otherwise quiet afternoon.

When people read about my husband Walter, they read that he is a beekeeper and love that tidbit of information. It suits their image of him. He, and Walter TY, are better bee men than I am a bee woman. Walter used to be the beekeeper and when he did it, he was very good. Quiet and gentle in his approach, he could work the bees. But he was not devoted. He would be interested for a moment, and then a film would call him and off he would go. He went away and was never to return—to them.

But, for the most part, the bees stayed, even though I am only a C-grade beekeeper. Don doesn't know about my low grade.

★ ★ ★

A year later, through my neglect of one queen or another, we need new bees again. This year, I was the one to collect the order of bees for Pete Horner and myself. The pickup point is in a parking lot, not yet taken over as prime real estate on the other side of the freeway, off Hamilton Park Drive between San Rafael and Novato. The truck was waiting with two men with a clipboard, a list, and hundreds of boxes of bees. At about $115 for each box, with extra queens, that truckload had to be worth close to $100,000. The men were rough woodsman types. One younger and in charge, the other a scrawny 110-pound, middle-aged woodsman with missing teeth, looking like any one of our street people but alive with edge and energy. Now that the truck was parked, many of the bees were flying freely, wondering if they were home now. They were buzzing around and around and making the first-time beekeepers nervous. The younger guy sold me an extra queen.

"Where shall I put her?"

"Put her up front with you. She'll like the company." He didn't say, "Don't put her in the back with the others. The bees will smell her and get confused by the smell of another queen."

So off I went to Skywalker Ranch. Leaving my box of bees in the car with the windows wide open, I took Pete's bees into the tech lounge to wait. It was an interesting moment of solitude, sitting in the lounge with its high ceiling and potted trees. In the middle of the afternoon, the lounge was deserted, all the Skywalker post-production worker bees busy with their computers in their own cells, only buzzing about when they needed to eat or scuttle to the bathroom. It was good to be quiet while

I waited for Pete, but I missed the sounds of laughter, comradeship, and lively discussion that bounced off the walls of older analogue film production. By the time Pete came from his own cell, a few bees had escaped and flown away, up into the light. I wondered how they would fare.

After these bees, I'll bring no more new things to the farm— for the moment.

White

White. As if with a trumpet blast, it is heralded by the spring blossoming of the Sally Holmes rose bursting into full bloom, hiding nests made by the hummingbirds and small finches. After the first burst, the rose bush follows through the summer, dipping long trailing arms forward into the flower bed beneath her, waving white blooms of remembrance—of Brian and the beauty of those lost boys and men. Later, just as summer sits down into the pasture dust, comes the arrival of a pristine, fresh white, covering the bare fields and then popping up anywhere it can in the gardens. First, the continual feverfew Tanacetum parthenium rises in tall clumps, all through the garden in every bed. Then—now—just as the feverfew is signing out its big summer push, along comes the chamomile, also of the daisy family Asteraceae, while holding on in the front border are low and tough clumps of white yarrow Achillea millefolium. These three are so similar in individual parts, yet very different in look. The feverfew gets tall and a little bit rough—almost aggressive—as those plants that reseed themselves do. When they brown up from the base and as the petals fade, they are easy to pull up. The chamomile hugs the ground more closely, the plants staying low in the soil, holding tight to the strong root clump while the stalks rise up and bobbling single blossoms call out, "Here I am, here we are!" The chamomile in the flower beds is fresh, green, healthy, and has dotted itself here and there, filling in bare holes. It will last awhile. There is much more in the fields, out along and in between the artichoke plants. It grows as if in rows itself. In the back field, which is dry, the chamomile looks like a rough-and-tumble country cousin to its suburban, house-bedded relatives. Along the driveway, the Romneya coulteri, California tree poppy, or fried egg plants dip and wave shyly from behind clumps of daisies and flowering artichokes. The white yarrow almost asks to be excused, so softly does it sit. The seasons are in motion as the moisture recedes, the wind teases, and the fog comes and goes on its own timetable.

Blackberries

In Sir David Attenborough's book *The Private Life of Plants*, he reminds us that in the right conditions, blackberries, Rubus rosaceae, can grow an inch a day. Found in the stomach of a Danish woman from over 2,500 years ago, it seems that blackberries have been a part of our diet since we and blackberries roamed together. For blackberries do roam, constantly surrounding us, a reminder that if we turn our back, leave for a week, month, or year, they will take over. Somehow, I take a strange comfort in thinking that maybe the blackberries will harbor life for renewal long after we have done our worst to the planet.

But now it is summertime and the farm berries, with no help from us, are ripening fast. The vines' roots reach down into the water table and find just what they need to produce big, juicy berries.

Basket after basket Walter brings me, until there is enough for jam, ice creams, pies, and our family favorite, Blackberry Surprise. Our family and friends, like almost everyone in West Marin, grew up picking these berries. A small simple task that is both a chore and a delight. And the rewards are great.

One year Clif Bar & Company based in Emeryville (how did they find us?) organized an outing for their employees at Blackberry Farm. It was to be a day of fresh air and exercise, cleaning bullrushes from the pond all morning before a long, lazy lunch on the porch with last year's home-brewed cider and ending with gallons of blackberry ice cream. A few weeks later, a couple of young employees returned, bringing a van full of youngsters from Oakland. Seeing them tumble out of the van, blinking in the sunlight and unsteady on their feet from the long, twisty drive, it was clear that a workday was not what these children needed. But, as we all do, they did need to feel useful. Out came bowls, jars, and anything that would hold berries. With a little direction here and there, they cautiously spread out across the fields, filling their bowls with berries, and their fingers becoming totally, appropriately, stained purple, along with their faces and shirts. After gathering them all back on the porch, it was time for lemonade and an hour of churning their berries into ice cream. They ate what they had harvested and made. I had to turn away and blink back tears as one girl looked into her bowl of berries and slowly said, "I've never seen a blackberry before."

Blackberry Surprise is another old 1960s recipe. This one is from our friend Pam Monson, who had a pottery studio on the mesa and a pottery shop in Stinson Beach that she ran with her husband Steve. Pam had made us a dish and included her family recipe in the box as a gift. Immediately, Blackberry Surprise became the farm's go-to-dessert with ice cream. In the fall of 1988 or '89, Walter, in an effort to keep the kitchen compost "looking tidy," would secretly disappear to Pam's studio for hours on end. There, he sat at the wheel and, under Pam's guidance, made a clay pot to hold the milk cartons we used for the kitchen compost. It was the best Christmas present, with a Lowly Worm—smiling, yes, smiling—handle for the lid. The square container and its lid graced the kitchen counter for many years before being overfilled once too often, and the lid fell off, shattering Lowly Worm. The square-etched container held on by the sink before retiring to a more seemly use as a flower vase. Looking back at Jerry Zucker's film *Ghost*, which Walter edited in 1990, the pottery scene still brings smiles of remembrance at the farm kitchen sink.

Then, there is a quick turn as the water recedes from the soil, the sun's warmth slackens, and the remaining berries redden but go no further. Some fall away, rotting on the vines, and the leaves curl as if discarding the fruit. The deer turn up their delicate noses and walk by, looking for something sweeter. As the Michaelmas daisies begin to bloom, most people turn away from foraging the hedgerows. But not Walter. Maybe it was in a moment of determination, thinking he would find blackberries and only finding the red, that the hunter in him would not come home empty-handed. Red berries he picked, and then red berry jelly for Thanksgiving he made.

Red Berry Sauce for Thanksgiving:

Makes about four 8 oz. jars.

- 8 cups prickly red berries, no green ones

- 4 cups sugar

- 3 cups cider vinegar

1. Boil together until solids are soft but not completely dissolved.

2. Strain out the last solids.

3. Then it is one-to-one sugar and liquid.

4. Bring to boil and stir as you do for jam. Use the old wooden spoon to drop test on a cold plate.

5. Pour into hot, sterile (sort of) jars and seal to set.

6. Lasts a long time, if not all eaten in the winter.

Chapter 9

Along the Flats: Falling in Love with Michael

Souvenir de Mme Léonie Viennot is a climbing rose that spreads alongside the front driveway fence, rising above my attempt at an herbaceous border, and the tall, loopy Cécile Brünners that embrace the back fences have crested. Following them is the tighter but still-rambling white rose, which interweaves with the pink rose on one side and a honeysuckle on the other. The house finches and hummingbirds build their nests within the rose branches, where they safely raise their broods all summer long. The empty nests are only discovered in the next spring's pruning.

It was some months after Brian, Michael Bernsohn's partner in life and the nursery, died that Michael came over from Las Baulinas Nursery and knocked on our door. He stood, grinning and clasping an overflowing one-gallon pot with this wonderful white rose. The small green leaves were healthy, bright, and shining with buds and blossoms of single white petals surrounding bright-yellow—orange, even—stamens and pistils pushing through. The rose was delicate yet sturdy, wild in its strength and is already in bloom while the farm roses are just beginning. Brian had taken cuttings from someone's garden and they had grown. This potted one was a gift from them both.

Michael and I sat on the deck in gratitude for each other, and thought of our friends, his partner Brian and my dressage teacher Ran Everett and his beloved partner Rod, with their beautiful smiles and who were no longer with us. The rose sat on the table, its white flowers peeking out of the green leaves like happy puppies. And we laughed again at that first cementing of our friendship.

★ ★ ★

Tentatively, he knocked on the glass window of the front door so as not to wake anyone, and would have turned away if I had not answered. But I did. Somehow, I had managed to stay awake. The house was quiet, the family all asleep. What excuse had I used to stay up after they had gone to bed? Maybe I had even said, "I'm going to the market with Michael," as if I was popping downtown for more milk at midnight.

Michael and Brian owned Las Baulinas Nursery at the corner where one finger road from the south met the other road from the north, and where there is a T-junction and stop signs. It is a low spot in the geography of the town, all roads gently slipping uphill from here. Pine Gulch Creek encircles the nursery and every winter overflows and floods the nursery grounds. Pumps and generators are a necessary part of the nursery equipment. But, somehow, it all survives. Michael and Brian lived in Stinson Beach, and Las Baulinas Nursery must have been such a special project for them both. You could feel their quiet determination and the horticultural love they brought to the nursery. Michael's passion for Italy and Italian gardens eventually led him on a whole new path of horticulture and landscape gardening, and he happily embraced anyone who shared his enthusiasm of discovery, the potential (unrealized for me) of a truly beautiful landscaped garden. Michael must have taken many like-minded souls with him on those solitary nighttime journeys. They were a rare treat to be gifted and shared, and when the invitation came my way, "Would you like to come to the flower market with me?" I had no hesitation and eagerly said, "Yes, please."

It was past midnight, now a Thursday morning, when that soft nighttime knock came on the door. The blue van was waiting, and I hopped in. Michael started the engine and drove slowly as we quietly left the farm. Then it began, this easy loving friendship that endures to today with a deep, simpatico understanding of each other and the way we need and choose to live.

Growing with the city of San Francisco in the later 1800s, the San Francisco Flower Market brought together the Italian, Chinese, and Japanese flower-growing communities and cultures within the Bay Area. Now a Japanese-American corporation, it is one of the last of five grower-owned wholesale flower markets in the country. Since 1956, the market has taken root at 6th and Brannan Streets, south of Market Street. Apart from commuting to the first American Zoetrope building at Fourth and Folsom, I didn't know what a world flourished in this southern part of town. But I was happy to explore with Michael. And hungry for a market. From pre-teen years, I had been drawn to the English cattle and livestock markets in nearby Guildford and Reading, adventuring and hitching rides with old haulers I knew from horse-barn and racing-stable days. What did they think of my friend and me, as they gently watched over us to see we came to no harm? And what did we learn from them beyond the memories of rough kindness? Later traveling in clusters of budding young-adult girls exploring the flower stalls of Covent Garden before wandering with Walter through flower and food stalls spilling over with fish, meat, wine, and cheese, and watching a lingering night turn to morning as Paris woke up at Les Halles. Those memories were long and deeply buried, but the thrill of market life remained.

Michael parked in his usual spot and we walked, making his rounds through the stalls, rows of pastels, rows of dark strong colors, more and more roses, Michael constantly gauging what to buy, how much, and from whom. It was always a guess, balancing the market, the budget, and the weekend customers back in his town. The sky was still dark when we left the market, the van now filled with bouquets of blooms and an attar of roses. Detouring through the San Francisco Conservatory gardens, we parked again to walk through the freshly filled flower beds, the moonlight playing on the blooms as they danced in reflection.

The drive home follows the moonlight, now bobbing on the water along the coast road. There is the beginning of light in the sky, but it is only the dawning of dawn. Michael drops me off at the farm driveway but doesn't come in. He goes on up the hill, where he can turn the van around and return down to the nursery. He will unload, leaving the flowers in their buckets before heading home. Later, when the nursery opens, he will have them ready for the weekend city customers who stop at the nursery on their way into town.

In the house, I go softly upstairs and slip into bed. There is a stir, and an arm reaches for me. With our ofttimes late returns, he from an editing bench, I from a bedside birth, we are comfortable falling asleep just as the day breaks.

Shittin' Chickens

Our neighbor Neshama's first gift to us was a small wooden hand-carved sign of Blackberry Farm that she had found in a rubbish pile. She dropped it by one day when she was walking to the Bolinas-Stinson School, where she then worked. It was the first of many years of "dropping it by" that happened between us. But this summer morning in 2014, Neshama phoned with a problem. Her daughter Melia, who lives in Oakland, had three old urban chickens and, due to life's changing circumstances, they needed a new home. Placing ads in the Oakland underground paper, her Facebook page, and other outlets had not yielded any takers.

"Call Aggie," begged Melia and so Neshama did, and I said yes, this being one of the moments when the universe has answered a question I was trying not to ask as I continued to mourn the loss of chickens. When the last bobcat attacked and clawed away the back of two small henhouses made for the teenage pullets 'safely' positioned in front of the farmhouses, killing the entire new flock of fifty hens, I admitted defeat—for a time. The coops were cut up for firewood, and since then the farm had had no chickens.

"There are three. One doesn't lay. You can do what you want with her."

I know, and they know, I won't kill her.

Half-heartedly, I am thinking about taking them to Sally or Rosie or even Mark, but full-heartedly, I am thinking, Do we have enough wire to make a run? Can handy Hector from downtown do it? Do I, should I, just get a made unit from the organic gardening corner at Tam Junction in Mill Valley?

Neshama drives up at 9 p.m. She is bone-weary and unloads two taped-together laundry baskets. Inside are the three chickens, silently huddled close to each other. We carry everything into the old tack room for the night and shut the door.

I wake up happy, and quickly remember why. Mitzi, a good-for-us kitty, is now a live-in, and we've just been gifted three old chickens. Soon I am outside setting up the old duck house with chicken food and fresh water. Then it is time to carry out the laundry basket cage. Neshama has done a great job of sealing their cage and it takes some serious work to open it up. In my pocket are three orange bird-banding rings. They have gone from my days of organized chicken husbandry to my beginning knitting projects, and now they are back for chicken banding. (What on Earth am I thinking, banding three chickens?) As I gently take each chicken out of the laundry hamper, I check her over and band her leg before putting her carefully in the dark duck house, but a scared chicken is a nervous chicken. The last chicken is the biggest; she is black and makes a terrible racket, putting up a huge struggle as I handle her before slipping her in to join her sisters. They are sex-links, hybrids bred for egg laying. The reds are scrawny and slim, but the black one is plumper. None of them have good feet; one toe and nail seem to be worn down on each foot.

For the first time in months, while out on my bike ride, I stop and pull handfuls of comfrey from the grass verge by Warren's field. I open the back of the duck house and put it in. The hens are huddled together by their food and make no effort to come to the greens. They make me smile. They are so very Oakland—urban, rough, and tough in their skittishness and scruffiness. I'm also realizing they are living just about where the old chicken house was when we first came to the farm. In 1973, Neshama's husband, John, gave us our first rooster, Horacio. He was the most ferocious rooster we ever had. Now it is Melia, John's daughter, who gives us our last hens in 2014.

So I can't help it. I buy a very expensive small, compact chicken house from the young organic gardener at Tam Junction. He drives into the farm with his coworker and they set to, putting it up for me. There is much squawking while I move the three hens over, but as soon as they move house, they are much happier. They will need to be let out often, as the hutch is really small. There are no eggs yet, but it has only been two days! There are three hens, as in a flock, from their perspective, so though the hutch is small, two would not be enough for them to feel they are a flock. There is no front gate on the hutch, so I worry if they will survive predators and the weather.

Free-range chickens are happier chickens and lay more nourishing eggs than those kept in cages. We all know that now. The question that remains for me is, what is the range on which the chickens are free? What is the relationship of snails, brown dirt, and green-plant growth to bright-yellow, protein-filled eggs? I think, and it is only my observation, that the relationship of green grasses to yellow yolks is important. That chickens that have free access to plants and grasses are far happier and lay brighter in every sense of the word, orange-yolked eggs if they can mix feed to their own desiring grit, bugs, and greens. Obviously, some breeds lay different-colored eggs. White Leghorns lay white-shelled eggs. Rhode Island Reds lay brown eggs. Araucanas lay white, blue, and pink eggs. One of the breeds I love the best is the French Maran, that lay the darkest of chocolate shelled eggs. I believe (I have to say that) plant chlorophyl is the most important ingredient for our chickens' health. Our three old ladies will lay good eggs. The eggs from Oak Mesa and Vanishing Point Ranch are as yellow-yolked as ours used to be. Why and how is that? Because they have a large, enclosed yard in which to roam. There is more than enough green and grit for them to get while still scratching into the dirt.

We have always kept chickens. The old chicken house that was waiting for us when we arrived was cleaned out of the Harvard student's papers and patched up for the incoming flock. That might have been our problem—the concept that a patched-up chicken coop would be enough to deter predators from taking our chickens. In England, it was the wily foxes, as big or bigger than a grand dame American raccoon and just as ferocious, who took away the hens, but here there are foxes, raccoons, and coyotes, the latter joined by bobcats.

Chickens and children go well together. Spring brings chick incubation to kindergarten and first-grade classes and boxes of day-old chicks to the post office. Our postmistress, Sharron, would listen to the peeps and phone their new homes before the post office opened. "Your chicks are here." There were more than a few of us who would hurry down and pick up our new babies. Sometimes there was a call from a city mother. "Aggie, Ginger was wondering if you could—?" And of course I could. So Henry the first arrived, with his sister Wisteria. Henry grew up to guard his flock, while Wisteria lived and laid eggs to the amazing age of seventeen.

While the apple trees were still so small and before Mickey began to plant crops between the trees, it was always a struggle to get in with the little tractor and mow, just enough to provide springtime pasture for the hens. But if I was late shutting them back in again, or was gone for a moment, there was a good chance that a hen would be missing by dusk.

On every returning to the farm I would try and try again, and learn new things with each rooster-led flock and breed.

Now, here was a little moment. Not serious chicken farming, just a few old ladies needing a home. But during the first week of being let out from their new henhouse, the girls had a bit of a fright. Since the goat man left the lower-back corner of the ranch up the hill (sadly dying of a heart attack alone in his little trailer), the bobcats have returned to a den at the bottom of the hillside behind us. They have been happy, as have we, with their diet of gophers, snakes, and rats, but once the three maids arrived, they knew. One afternoon, a bobcat came down from the back hills to check out the noise and the smell. She crept closer and closer—just looking, mind you. But the cluck-cluck of a quick take-away supper proved too much. A creep, a pause before the pounce, and one hen was grabbed by the neck and off they went. Luckily, it was a teatime moment and I heard the squawk. Leaping out of my chair with a yell and through the French doors, I was greeted with the suspended still silence of the hunt. There was only the view of a swinging bird behind the far side of the plum tree trunk and an angry twitch of a bobcat tail from this side. Another shout and, with great reluctance, the bobcat leapt forward, dropping our little red hen as she jumped the picket fence and slipped away. I bent over the hen who, though cyanotic, was, miracles of miracles, still breathing. I picked her up, brought her inside, and put her on my lap where she sat after her very nasty turn. Slowly, she opened and blinked her eyes as I drank my tea for both of us. An hour later, I suggested she join her friends. She was not keen at all, but I put her back outside and left the dining-room door open.

As dusk fell, one by one, the girls all filed inside and squeezed themselves between the door and Granny's drinks cabinet. "We will be just fine here in the dining room," they seemed to clearly say. But I shooed them back out and into their pen and piled bigger, heavier logs around the edge.

There was no scratching and scraping last night. Our three little Oakland maids may still manage, if I can let them out in the afternoon and evenings when I am working outside. They look happy running, with that funny little hop they have, from under the plum tree to clumps of fresh grass. Scratching and grabbing at bugs and worms as they uncover them. The one egg laid every other day still gives me a thrill.

It has been several weeks now since the bobcat came to visit. But the girls still question every teatime if they cannot, just for tonight, camp by Granny's cocktail cabinet. While they hover closer, they leave their mark clearly on the back porch, in case I should forget they are there.

Mickey has been losing hens all year. The bobcat's young family raised in their den behind our field may have left home and moved across the street and down the road. The coyote, whose den was farther up the hill, also moved on to other pastures and henhouse opportunities. The foxes have now moved in, happy with the smaller rodents but still watchful for easier pickings.

The Gospel Flat Farms flock is a mixture of breeds. Only a few are "pretty" in the ornamental sense and there are a lot of White Leghorns to keep production up. We are unkind in our rather snobby attitude to the work of the little white hen and should honor the tough little Leghorn more. The eggs from Mickey's are a good mixture of white, pink, and brown, and maybe people will stop turning their noses up at the white eggs when they see these all together. The Leghorn hen lays and lays for us, but because she and her eggs are white, we often dismiss her and her eggs as boring. Truthfully, she lays better and works harder than any little red hen. She puts the Rhode Island Red and New Hampshire Brown and Black breeds to shame. The Wyandotte hens work hard, but cannot compete with the steady production of the Leghorns.

Soon I will have to leave again. I am blessed to have so many people to love in my life but the pulls and heartaches of leaving one for the other remain as strong as ever. And I am blessed to have friends offering to take these three ladies and give them "forever" homes. Will we ever be home long enough for us to have a real flock of hens again? I would love that, but it is hardly safe anymore. The brush that has taken over the hillside behind us and surrounds all the farms is such a mixed blessing. It provides habitat for wildlife—and provides habitat for wildlife.

Conscious animal husbandry is hard. Where I grew up in England, there used to be a real butcher in Odiham Village. Farmers would drive small lorries, carrying their livestock up to his back door. The sheep, pigs, and goats would be taken in and dispatched with very little delay or disruption or fear. Later, they would reappear as fine cuts of meat displayed in the High Street front window.

Piers Plowright, a renowned BBC radio documentary producer, and a friend and fine mentor to those of us who love radio drama, once made a radio piece entitled *The Pig Man*. It featured remembrances of the post-war families who kept a pig in the back garden of the small shallow slum-city streets for nine months long, growing their spring piglet to winter barrow. Every day the housewives of the street brought their kitchen scraps and full slop pails to feed the pigs.

We kept and used to kill our chickens. It is difficult to look in the eyes of an animal you are about to kill. I can't do it anymore, and I eat a lot less chicken and meat than I used to.

Bill Niman knows their beef is not tainted because he tracks his livestock from farm breeding, birth, and growth to slaughter. That truth is written on his face and is the pain we see on many ranchers' faces. If the rancher trucks his stock in and follows them to slaughter, there has to be an acceptance of birth, growth, and death that is ancient and necessary if we are to eat meat mindfully.

Mickey Springs a Leak

Irrigation lines come in all sizes. Star Route Farms uses big metal pipes for overhead irrigation. They used to pull the water from Pine Gulch Creek but now a big reservoir has been built; it is supposed to be guarding and monitoring the agricultural water use by Star Route Farms, Paradise Valley, and Martinelli's. Paradise Valley mostly uses sturdy large piping; the funky plastic tubing is used by smaller farmers. Each has its advantages and disadvantages. It takes a lot of time to move those big, long, metal pumping pipes by men and machines from acre to acre. But the row crops can be flooded into attention and grow fast enough to be harvested before the crawling bugs or swooping crows have a chance to devour the tender young plants. The strong metal and plastic pipes also take time to assemble, place, and adjust, as well as moving them from crop to crop, rotating the plumbing along with the fresh plantings. The same is true for the buried, lighter plastic pipes, which are good for smaller acreage or for a farm where the water is limited and timers are needed to regulate flow and usage. There is some safety in burying the plastic, but sometimes the water pressure burps with such force that it splits the older plastic and the water pours forth in seeming flatulent relief.

Somewhere, in more scholarly writings, there are studies on the rate and effect of water on organic farms in relation to the soils and microclimates of the areas. Water needs to be as balanced as the nutritional input. Given to excess, water will urge crops to grow so fast that they come to maturity quickly, looking full, fresh, and unblemished. Pests don't stand a chance, but these crops can be lacking in nutrients and flavor. Water withheld makes the plants work hard, struggle for maturity. Blemishes show, pests take advantage, and growth is slow.

Irrigation and water management are a fine balancing act of husbandry and business.

When you are an arable farmer with many growing areas and / or extensive acreage, watching the water pipes is as much a responsibility as checking livestock is for the animal farmer. Sometimes we miss some catastrophic event—a cow stuck in a ravine, a ewe struggling with a twin birth, or a burst pipe.

One morning, when I went out to harvest more early windfalls from the apple orchard, I luckily tripped over the split hosepipe by the gate. A couple of hours before or afterwards and I might have missed it, the water flowing freely and draining our well.

The water hiccupped and moved around my pointless fix. Duct tape doesn't hold water. A quick bicycle ride down to Gospel Flat Farms and the message relayed. Mickey came quickly, took a look, disappeared, and returned with the right tools and tape. It took him five minutes, ten if you count the driving back and forth, and the hose was fixed.

The winter squash that lay between the apple trees quickly perked up again as their water supply resumed. The bright-yellow blossoms turned upward once more while the huge weary leaves continued their carpeting of the orchard. The bees are busy with pollination and soon we will see budding winter squash on the ground as the ripening apples bend the tree boughs to welcome them.

Sherman Comes Home

Sherman Smith and his siblings were raised by their grandmother, Juana Briones, in the farmhouse that is now home to our family. Juana was the granddaughter of the renowned Juana Briones of San Francisco and, like her grandmother, was a strong matriarch of this country branch of the family. She owned the lower belt of the flats up to the mesa where it was bordered by the Tacherra family ranch. Slowly, the Briones land was nipped and tucked into smaller parcels until, by the time of Sherman's grandmother, it was down to a few hundred acres. Sherman, like most men of his Coast Miwok heritage, was a natural-born horseman. He spent much of his youth managing the downtown stables and horse teams that pulled wagons of visitors across the mountain to town.

Sherman was a constant fixture at the biweekly Bolinas Rod and Boat Club Pancake Breakfasts, where the men cooked and served and the women (those allowed) cleaned up after them. Slowly, this changed as the men got old and occasionally forgetful, and their women stepped in and covered for them. A timid friendship bloomed between our children and Sherman. He knew they were living in the house he had grown up in.

Sometimes we are lucky and learn each other's stories; other times we go blindly about our own business not knowing. Why, for instance, did Sherman always take the Sharpie pen he used for writing our breakfast orders and then dot black marker faces on the little hands holding the railing by the counter? It wasn't until years later that we stumbled across the grave, way in the back of the Bolinas Cemetery, of Sherman's four-year-old son.

And then Sherman got sick. He was no longer able to ask, "What are you having, young man?" on Sundays. Somewhere a stool was found for him in the kitchen, and he would sit by

Ed Letter, listening to the orders and talk while the bacon sizzled and pancakes were flipped. Soon, even that became too much for him, and the kitchen stool was conspicuously empty of his presence. Sherman was to be seen, though, maybe even more than before, as he drove his truck downtown, parked across from the gas station, and sat in the cab for an hour or two, watching the comings and goings of the town. Old friends would stop for a few minutes on their way to and from the post office and hardware and grocery stores. New friends would chat too, and often, on one of those days, we spoke. He had seen we were working on the farm and I asked if he would like to come over and take a look. The twinkle returned to his eyes, and that afternoon, Sherman Smith came to visit. Slowly, he drove his gray truck into the driveway. He carefully slid out of the cab and looked up at his old home. We climbed the steps onto the rickety porch and went inside.

"Yes, it was like this. That old heater is gone. It was a monster. Kitchen stove still works, then?"

"Would you like to see upstairs? Nothing is finished."

He nodded and reached for the stair knob he had known all his life and held on tight. He would need all his strength to make it up those stairs again.

"That was my room, on the left."

"It's our son's room now."

"Bitter cold, it was."

"Bitter cold, it still is." We laughed as we slowly went up the stairs.

Sherman grew up on this farm in that bitter cold room, along with his brothers. Their parents lived in the farm next door, now the Franklin Farm. It is hard to tell from old photographs of Gospel Flats which farmhouse was built first. The pictures show one story but Sherman told another and, for whatever reason, the children were raised here. During the 1906 earthquake, the kitchen chimney had fallen on Grandma Juana Briones's head. But she was all right, apparently. The family were known to be rowdy, playing the ukulele on the upper balcony.

After showing him the bare bones of what we had begun upstairs, we went back down and walked around the outside of the farmhouse.

"The pear tree is a delight. Tell me about the pear tree."

Sherman looks at it and smiles an I-remember-when smile. It is almost a chuckle, and I think that this is the happiest I have seen him for months. He looks up into its branches. There is a breeze and the young leaves are healthy as they flutter towards him. It is summer, Sherman's last on this Earth, and the budding pears helped draw the limbs forward, bowing in remembrance of things past for him, waving hello and farewell.

"There was a big storm in the '50s. The gully broke at the back and mud poured down from the hill. Came all through here, a terrible mess for both farms. Took a long time to clear it all up." The big rain had stormed through a gully behind the two ranches. The overgrown gully now falls directly behind the line between the Franklin Farm and Blackberry Farm, and in a big storm, more overgrown brush could fall, burst, and flood the fields again. The pear tree must have been planted by the Peterses, after the cleanup of the mud and whatever else slid down the hillside in that storm over sixty years ago.

We talked more about the tree.

"We think it is a Louise Bonne de Jersey."

Sherman smiled and shrugged. The variety of pear tree was not much interest to him. It was a good tree, with tasty and useful fruit. Hardy as a farm tree needs to be, a working tree. It cheered everyone up. We walked around outside a little bit more, but Sherman was tired. The climb up and down the stairs had drained his energy, and he needed to rest. He could go home now. All was right. The farm was safe, growing, changing, and happy.

Louise: A Good Name for a Pear

When we first came to the farm in 1972, we didn't pay a lot of attention to the pear tree. It was very nice; pretty in spring, and yielded a good crop of pears in autumn. The tree seemed happy and healthy. Then the horses began to produce more manure than I knew what to do with and I was raking the fields as well as the barn, mounding manure into piles. Only then did I start to feed the manure to the pear tree, along with the other fruit trees, vegetable plots, and flower beds. The manure got spread on anywhere that might be, and anything that was, growing on the farm. And everything loved it.

When Jeff Creque showed up at the farm with his red truck in the early '80s, I knew I had met a kindred spirit. Almost weekly, Jeff would come down to the farm with Susan Englebry, and load up with the rich straw manure to feed the Commonweal garden he was bringing back to life. Between us, we kept the pile from steaming and catching fire, though often, the pitchfork would dig into a new hatching of bright red squiggly worms and we would both smile. One noontime, talking across the manure pile as we used to do, I told him how wonderful our pear tree was. When Jeff finished loading his truck, he rammed his pitchfork into the mound of manure and we walked around to the side of the house so I could show off the tree. He stood still about ten feet away and studied her, slowly smiling as he took in the healthy shiny leaves and slow-growing fruit. Eventually, he couldn't help himself and grinned with glee.

"It is so healthy. It looks fantastic."

And it was and it did. But what variety was it? Some kind of a Bosc was as close as I had come. Jeff went back to his books and began his kerosene-lit evenings searching for our tree. When he returned the next week, he had a name.

"I think it is the Louise Bonne de Jersey." Looking at all the evidence, we agreed this was who she was. Jeff fell in love with the tree. He took scion and grafted several trees onto root stock for the Commonweal garden, where the trees thrived long past his stewardship.

The pear tree seemed to have been biding its time, patiently waiting for us, and the next year, after we started to feed it the manure, it gathered a new strength, cropping both flower and fruit heavily. Louise Bonne de Jersey is the perfect tree for us, for the farm and the microclimate in this corner of the flats. The blossoms were a gift of spring that decorated the altar of St. Aiden's church for the Easter celebration. The pear harvest begins on the Labor Day weekend and continues for a good month. The crown crop is left for the crows. I began to bottle the pears for the winter in the same way my mother had. In those early days, almost all West Marin women canned, preserved, and shared our bounty, and some of us still do. It is a welcome soothing chore and, for me, the habit is hard to break. Our girls would pluck pears from their bedroom window, just for the delight in it. When Chris Giacomini first began selling organic produce at Toby's Feed Barn, I took the pears to him and he sold them easily from the feed barn. Gaining courage to branch out, I went to the Bolinas People's Store, where they were devoured. In later years we would sell these pears at Stellina Restaurant, Shorty's Produce at Perry's Deli, The Farm Stand, and restaurants in Marin and Berkeley, even occasionally to Chez Panisse. Each year, the pear tree was fed manure, and each year she produced more and more fruit. One year I estimated that we harvested five hundred pounds off that one brave tree.

In the autumn of 2004, we were asked by our neighbor to contribute a basket of pears that they could send to New York where their friend, President Bill Clinton, was recovering from quadruple-bypass heart surgery. It was fun to put together a beautiful basket of pears, still firm, giving them time to ripen on their way across the country. I hope the patient enjoyed them.

More excitingly, Jeff began to teach me to graft and, finally I was successful with one small pear tree. We planted the young tree in the apple orchard, where it flourished. In its first adolescent year, the tree produced a few pears that weighed almost a pound each before disaster struck in the form of a big old grandpa gopher who ate the roots. Gone, done, death.

In the early 2000s, Steve Quirt, who worked with Marin County agriculture education, came to visit the farm. He too marveled at the pear tree and suggested we grow more of them.

"Orchard trees need three things: water, feeding, and protection from predators. They can manage with two of the three but not with only one."

It was good advice that I struggled to heed. He set me on an unwinnable war with terrorist gophers. Even with an extra SWAT team of badgers moving into the orchard, the gophers remain and will strike, bringing down a favorite tree with ease.

★ ★ ★

For the first time in its long life, the pear tree is definitely ill. What I thought of as one broken branch that I must get to soon has become a mass of dying branches. A couple of apple trees have had it. Some survived after a lot of heavy pruning and others didn't. The pear tree will need one whole day and an old tarpaulin, the ladder, and every handsaw I have—patience and time—and then to be fed with the remaining manure. Maybe fed even more later, but for now make up for the last few years of half-hearted care. Poor tree. It was still producing until a few years ago, when it began to change. First it sent up really tall growth spurs to reach for the sun that was being blocked by the upstart silver birch and quince trees now crowding the pear.

After the horses left, I had to ration the manure, and travel took me away at crucial times. The brave old pear tree went without its manure feedings for one or two years, then suddenly, it sickened. A little less fruit last year and a full-blown polka-dot smattering of fire blight this year. Foolishly, I hoped it was just windburn, but soon it became unmistakable—disease had struck the leaves and spurs and some of the smaller branches.

This weekend, Walter TY was free and offered to help prune the diseased limbs off the tree. We worked steadily for several hours and managed to cut away nearly all the fire blight. It is binned up, ready to go away. There is just a little more to take off the top, which he will do from Carrie and Connie's old bedroom window.

I will feed the tree the last of the manure and then ask Don Murch to deliver fresh from Vanishing Point Ranch for the winter feeding. But since the cost of keeping horses and ponies has outstripped most family budgets, the supply of fresh horse manure from Sally's ranch is smaller and mostly taken by those farmers who can easily haul it away.

For a few years, while we were in London with Walter editing *Coup 53*, the farmhouse became The Gentleman's Club, and Sasha Gold was a long-term guest as he continued with his studies. Among his many skills, Sasha is a talented and gifted arborist. His room on the farm was our girls' old room, the one that overlooked the pear tree. Between bouts of very serious study, Sasha couldn't help but see the pear tree's plight and he took it to heart. Pruned and treated by Sasha, the pear tree is flourishing once more.

And a Memory

My father was big—standing, even when elderly, just below his youthful height of six-foot-three. Late in life, he was bowled out by love and love led him, like a busy bower bird, to create a comfortable yet elegant Edwardian country home with his beloved partner at his side. Beauty and function were intertwined for him. It was a typical wartime, self-sufficient country home and there were a lot of vegetables. And fruit. The brick wall that flanked the kitchen garden on two sides reflected the weak sunlight that was all most of England garnered in the summer months of the middle of the twentieth century. In this section of the kitchen garden, he also grew his dessert apple and pear trees. My father was of grandfatherly age when I was born and, as a young child, from late summer through the winter, each morning we walked together slowly to the bottom of the garden and chose half a dozen apples and four pears to bring into the kitchen for the week.

The dessert pears were brought to the dining room where the Crown Derby bowl sloped to caress these gifts of autumn. After my nursery supper and before our evening time together, my father would stop and linger at the sideboard to cradle a pear in his hand. Gently, with his now-soft, old fingers, he would press the neck of a pear to test its ripeness, and smile. "You have to stay up all night to taste a pear at perfection."

I would nod, only knowing that a pear was sweet with juice that dribbled down my chin and had to be wiped away with a napkin and a smile.

Chapter 10

A Mixed Melody of Fruits and Films

Blueberry Trials

My friend and author Gail Reitano is writing an essay on blueberries for a journal article. Now she has asked me to write something too, a sort of research exercise for us both. I love blackberries but hardly know blueberries. In the spirit of more research, Gail and her husband Nick took an adventure to a farm up north of Tomales to hand-pick their own berries. Gail came back with a basket for me just in time for a taste test with organic blueberries from the grocery chain Mollie Stone's, which were very different. Mollie Stone's were not bigger but were more juicy; sweet, but not really "that" blueberry flavor. Gail's hand-picked berries are full of flavor but are tart, as if something doesn't agree with the plants: geography, soil, climate, and, yes, water. Even with root irrigation, I expect the soil composition does not come close to the East Coast pine-barren forests and peat bogs, and there may lie in the East—and lack in the West—the real blueberry flavor.

★ ★ ★

Through the spring and summer of 1979, Walter and the post-production crew were finishing the soundtrack mix of *Apocalypse Now*. There was a premiere release in New York at the end of August. The fever pitch of those months took no prisoners. So I took five children to the Canadian uncles, aunts, and cousins Murches' lakeside cottage at Honey Harbor on the Georgian Bay in Ontario. Walter TY's friend, eleven-year-old Nick, was on his first trip away from home in England, and my heart still aches to know the fear he must have felt upon landing. I had muddled the dates and there was no one to meet him when he arrived in Toronto. I put it down to a moderate case of living with the fever of *Apocalypse Now*. But Aunt Phyllis finally gathered us all up safely at her home in Toronto before sending us on our way the next day. We took the bus north and scrambled out to be greeted by cousin Philip at the harbor for the boat ride across the lake. As the boat pulled up to the dock, six-year-old Beatrice leapt out, stripping off her clothes, and ran up onto the shore. Back she ran toward us and down the dock, shining in her bright-green swimsuit, and jumped into the lake. She couldn't swim, but bounced on the lake bottom, and we, all still in the boat, caught her on the rebound. There were three cottages discreetly built each away from the other, on the rocky outcrop owned by Aunt Phyllis's family. We walked the trail, packing in all we had brought, through to the end cottage that was waiting for us.

Our task for the summer was to build a septic tank. Each child brought ten rocks from the lakeside to the pit before breakfast. That tank is still working more than forty years later. We had brought provisions suitable for camp life, and every other day, Aunt Phyllis or cousins Philip and Stephen would motor me across the lake to small stores to add to the larder the basics needed to feed five hungry children. I learned to be ever grateful for the wonder of Wonder Bread. After breakfast, there was swimming and fishing. After lunch, there was blueberry gathering in the woods, led by knowledgeable Stephen. We would all pick a small cluster here, a bigger bounty there, harvesting what we could in competition with the bears and woodland creatures. The berries were small, tart, and sweet at the same time. Those are the berries I remember when I think of blueberries. Woodland berries, harvested in small clusters from resilient shrubs amidst familial friendship, as this generation of Canadian Murches and their young second cousins from California learned about and from each other. The children were a jolly band in those weeks, and the silence from the West Coast was bearable during the day. It was only when the starlight flickered on the lake as it rippled in the nighttime summer breeze that I felt the chill and was afraid.

★ ★ ★

Then, in 1986, Walter and Walter TY flew east to rent and fill a truck with some stored family furniture and Walter Tandy Murch's paintings. Stopping somewhere in New Hampshire, they picked four punnets of blueberries and drove on for three days with the berries on ice. It was late evening when they pulled into the farm and wearily, but proudly, got out of the truck. Laying the remaining two baskets of berries down on the kitchen counter, the elder said, "Make me a pie the way my father made it." I had never made a blueberry pie before, but whatever I did, the pie tasted of blueberries. With obligatory ice cream, it finished a sweet welcome-home family supper.

I asked Gail, whose grandfather was a blueberry farmer, for a family recipe for blueberries. And she gave me this blueberry tea cake, which has been among her family favorites since the 1960s.

Baking it, I realized how much of our comfort food comes from when, as new mothers, we were first baking for our young children. It makes me think about how much we bring forward from our own mothers. This cake is the perfect mid-morning or late-afternoon tea cake. Is it the genesis for the muffins of today?

Blueberry Tea Cake:

Yields 12 medium-sized squares.

- 2 cups unbleached flour (240 g)

- 2 teaspoons baking powder

- ½ cup natural sugar (100 g)

- ¾ cup milk (180 ml)

- 2 cups blueberries (300 g)

- 1 egg

- ¼ cup (½ stick / 55 g) unsalted butter

Preheat oven to 350°F (175°C).

1. Butter an 8-inch (20 cm) square pan.

2. Cream the butter and sugar.

3. Add egg, milk, flour, and baking powder alternately, and mix until smooth.

4. Fold in blueberries. Spread the batter in the pan, and sprinkle with cinnamon.

5. Bake for 35 minutes.

Returning To and From *Oz*

It began, as things did in the 1980s, with a phone call, a summons to meet with a new young executive (of what? Did it say on his business card?), Tom Wilhite at Disney. Fresh suits at Disney must have had a meeting, making lists of untapped talent that wouldn't cost too much but had an interesting track record. As if at a horse auction, Walter was brought into the sales ring and appraised. Tom asked Walter what he might be interested in that would suit Disney. When Walter replied the *Oz* books, Tom sat up a little straighter, as Disney owned them all, something Walter did not know, and those movie rights were about to expire. Walter chose *The Marvelous Land of Oz* and *Ozma of Oz* on which to base his screenplay. Disney calls it *Return to Oz* and Walter asked his writing pal Gill Dennis from *The Black Stallion* to join him on this new adventure.

When the children returned from school at 3 p.m. to be greeted with the smell of cigars and whiskey in the kitchen, they knew Uncle Gill had arrived. For a few days, the house would ring with barking laughter as Gill recounted stories of his Hollywood life. The *Oz* schedule was a little different from *The Black Stallion*; the green light of a go production still pulsed unsteadily, but the stakes seemed higher as Walter was to direct their story. For months, the script was passed from one to the other as it was hammered out and kneaded into shape.

Walter had read Beatrice all his childhood *Oz* books. Night after night, they were tucked up in her room as the tales from *Oz* unfolded. For Bea, it was magical—and somehow for Walter too—but I could make no sense of *Oz*. When the children watched the 1939 film *The Wizard of Oz*, I would find ways to leave the room, returning to the kitchen or the barn. Each child grows through the stories of their time and culture. I understood the make-believe reality of *The Wind in the Willows* but not *The Wizard of Oz*. Walter and Bea read on.

But it still took Walter a while to get started writing his first draft. Then there was another phone call, this time from Jerry Richardson, a riding and Pony Club chum. He had come across a piece of machinery in an antique shop in San Anselmo. As much as the machine itself, he was caught by the tag: *Sold— Murch. Deposit paid $25.* Was that us? It was us—or rather, Walter. He had seen the machine, been drawn to it, put a deposit down, and then ran out of dollars and memory. With a birthday around the corner, I took the saved $100, earmarked for the dentist, and brought it home.

As Walter looked at the machine, it looked back at him. Its metallic face became clear, along with its horror, for this machine was a prototype of an early American electrotherapy treatment. Now, Walter and Gill began in earnest to write the story taking place on a struggling farm, with chickens and a girl who could not sleep. Did the chickens who clucked in and out of our barn under the office cluck their way from the *Oz* books into the barn and back into the script pages?

For months, the script was written, rewritten, slashed to reemerge again, until the green light glowed steadily and we packed up to leave our home for another two years in England. Walter was gone a lot; there were meetings in Los Angeles, then location scouting in Europe and North Africa. I was caught between having to plan for two years away from the farm and the knowledge that all of this could come to nothing with just another meeting and phone call.

Our four children were older and progressing as they should, but somehow this disruption in our lives brought about the beginning of a barely suppressed panic for me. Carrie was on her way, working as a makeup artist and Sassoon-trained hairstylist. Connie was to spend one year in the California Conservation

Corps, following Walter TY and Bea, who had put in their Corps months. Walter TY was at boarding school in Danville and would join us for vacations, while Bea would come with us to England, bringing her open heart to embrace Fairuza Balk and Emma Ridley, who were to live out her dreams. Bea would spend the weekdays in Hampshire living with my mother, her granny, while attending my old school, St. Nicholas, thirty years after I had, and wearing the same school uniform. It felt like a shredding of the family we had woven together.

The biggest question was of what to do with the house. Another phone call—this time from Don Deane.

"I've met the new vicar coming for St. Aidan's Church and he wants to live in town. How about he takes over the farm while you are gone?"

As in many tiny communities, the town is top-heavy with churches with low attendance that struggle to find a willing shepherd for their flock. The pickings are slim; maybe an elderly pastor retiring from a larger congregation, or someone who needs a placement for one reason or another. But Don seems to like this new man. Could this be an answer to a prayer or too good to be true? Don gathered us seemingly more-churchy-than-hippie mothers together to meet this soon-to-be new member of the community. But quickly, through us all, an uneasiness spread. Together we whispered, not too quietly, and found he had, one by one, hit on every one of us, making overtures that were seriously unbiblical in appropriateness and made our collective flesh crawl. Carrie and Connie added their tales to ours. The vicar was camping in the hayloft above the barn, waiting until we moved out of the farmhouse, and it was my place to speak up.

"If your actions and words make our girls feel uncomfortable, then they must stop."

But it was too late to change plans and, with that warning in place, we could only hope he would behave.

Those same beloved friends helped me pack and, as we drove out of town, they stood by the school with a big banner and balloons, waving to us, wishing us luck. We were too wrapped up in this adventure to understand we were carrying their hopes and dreams with us as we turned onto Route One, through the city to the airport.

And the vicar? It was left to our neighbor, Perry Fly, to take care of him. Perry was then best known for keeping an immaculate tool shed and giving advice on parking. Venturing into middle age, he had now taken a bride, who one evening he found basking in their hot tub—with the vicar. Perry did the only sensible thing under the circumstances. Dashing back to their house, he grabbed his shotgun and, raising it into the sky, let rip a couple of rounds, shooting his anger at such betrayal into the air. The vicar leapt from the tub like a startled goblin protecting his soft manhood as best he might, and fled, taking Perry's new wife with him.

Carrie, Connie, and Walter TY all dipped in and out of London during those two long years. When Carrie visited the set, she easily flitted from one executive to another. Connie arrived bruised and crushed, after learning that her Corps coworkers were stealing money from her. Walter TY arrived with his friend Chris Monson and a huge headache, to explore the city of London. A headache at sixteen years old: was that from a boozy night out before flying, the beginning of infectious mononucleosis, or was this small pulsing, a little brain tumor making itself known for the first time? We never even considered the last option. The boys set out exploring, learning how to navigate a city.

I went to the studio every day with Walter. "What to do with Aggie" must have been a question he wrestled with until he came up with "the nurse." Driven by beloved Mac, who was to remain a lifelong friend, we arrived at the studio together in the morning. Walter headed off to meetings and various offices, while I went straight to the set, taking up my nursing place with the firemen and the carpenters. The men on the floor accepted me easily and, finding I had only an old soft shooting bag of my father's and not a proper first-aid box on which to sit, the carpenters quickly made me one, which they all signed. Immediately, a memo was sent down from the middle-management team: "No personal carpentry to be done on set." But they were too late.

When the guard at the stage door began calling out, "Good morning, Sister," the greeting reserved for an English hospital-ward charge nurse, I knew I was safe. Most of the work was to be vigilant and careful. I watched how much the young actors and gymnasts worked before it was break time, and there were some stitches for a stunt double in the water. Then, close to the end of shooting, holding a blood-pressure clinic for seven hundred cast and crew during the three days of the Emerald City set, and finding a production designer who needed to be sent straight to his doctor. Friday, the last day of shooting, and at the cast-and-crew wrap party—where the exhaustion and relief were fueled with alcohol and jazz—it was time to thank those wives and girlfriends who had stayed home alone, managing their families, keeping suppers warm, and sending partners off to work in the dark. The following morning, the head carpenter phoned me in tears. His elbow was deeply paining him and he was booked for surgery on Monday. He had worked on the film for two years and didn't want it to end. We stayed on the phone until his tears were spent.

The five-month shooting schedule had been long and brutal. Back at Disney, Tom Wilhite, the first executive with whom Walter met, had been replaced by Richard Berger. Even an early-evening gathering in London with Roy Disney was now a dim memory. As each consecutive producer came on board, they swept clean the desk of those half-completed projects before them. Gary Kurtz had been brushed aside by Paul Maslansky. Hot from his *Police Academy* box-office success, Paul answered to Richard Berger and not Roy Disney. Five weeks into the schedule, Walter was fired by Berger at Maslansky's instigation. After taking Walter home and to bed, I was asked to take Richard out for dinner. Mac drove me and waited outside our favorite old English hotel while I listened to Richard talk on and on of his affection and admiration for Walter. As I pushed my food around my plate, it sulked and congealed into a cold greasy heap. I sipped the bitter wine slowly and felt like a call girl on overtime.

The weekend was hard and passed in a dream. And in that dream came the reality of George Lucas flying in from Japan and guaranteeing the film's completion. Walter was immediately rehired and returned to the set five days later. When the shooting was over and Paul Maslansky was gone, the beloved Robert Watts came on board as a real producer to finish the film. Francis Coppola flew in next. After watching some of the shot footage in the screening room, he walked over to Paul in the dark, leaned close, and told him, "Touch my face. Touch my face. Those are real tears." It was Francis at his finest.

During the next tumultuous weeks, film directors who had suffered many of the same pressures as Walter came to stand by his side. Those close friends, George and Francis, were followed by Steven Spielberg, Phil Kaufman, and Irvin Kershner, all enjoying the extreme discomfort their presence brought to Paul Maslansky before his bags were packed.

Return to Oz was still in post-production when Jeffrey Katzenberg strutted into the boardroom on the tailcoat of Michael Eisner in 1984. Eisner was ready to close the chapter on this project and Katzenberg went through the motions of preview screenings in California. The last was held in San

Francisco and followed by lunch for filmmaker friends only. No Disney executives were invited and that snub was felt by them. In George's dining room, this band of brothers gathered around Walter and, as they all have always done for each other, advised and supported him, giving him the courage to jump this last hurdle. And the women? Twelve of us were outside the dining room, perched on the hallway stairs. I saw the skills we each had let grow fallow, supporting the art of our husbands and lovers. Linda Ronstadt was the only one on those stairs who had kept her dreams and gifts alive, and maybe that was enough. Meanwhile, Jeffrey Katzenberg used the new stiff-bristled broom handed to him by Michael Eisner with fierce efficiency. With no thought given to publicity, it took him no time to sweep *Return to Oz* away and by the time the film was released, it was all over.

The gift of such a journey is the strength of love and friendship shared between friends of the film and home communities. Two years later, the same friends who had waved us goodbye welcomed us home again, helped to scour-clean the house and throw the mattress out from the fornicatingvicar (all one word). *Return to Oz* had come and gone, disappearing with hardly a trace in the three weeks from its opening to our returning home from England and *Oz*. Reviews panned it and it was hard to read what they had written.

It took longer for Walter and the film to recover. Over the forty years since its release, *Return to Oz* has developed a strong cult following, and Walter an even bigger one.

Russian Doll Memories

Like Russian matryoshka dolls, memories can get folded one within another through five ages of womanhood: the grandmother enfolding the mother, enfolding the woman, the child, and babe, yet visible in each is their strength and vulnerability. Memories are buried and hidden as life adds another one to stack on top, to cover or smother the memory laid down before. But if one layer gets lifted, there lies the next and then another underneath and, if we are not careful, they will come again, asking to be acknowledged, looked at, and even accepted in a new way.

And when I think about finding Ali in the barn early in the morning, I wonder why I return to that memory so often. Maybe I am curious as to where this will lead—further back than I think I can go again. For Ali reminds me of me...

In 1995, Walter is happily in Rome. He is part of a multinational production team and has an editing crew of English and Italians whom he loves dearly, and a project, *The English Patient*, that will prove challenging. We are not sure how long we will be apart. He will be engrossed in the work with his team, and I am caught with the excitement of birthing a new community radio station. And while still a part of the KPFA Pacifica Drama and Literature Department, I am also gleaning programs for our new small, tiny-at-the-moment station-that-could. Next up in the studio is Sir David Attenborough with his new book, *The Private Life of Plants*. I'm more than on home ground and the book is a breeze for me. Sir David is a good old pro. *The Private Life of Plants* appears almost a knockoff for him, a quick fill-in between bigger projects with which to keep him busy. Sir David is still cresting his prime, always on the go, happily absorbed in his passion. I know the type. I think he finds me a bit of a relief as he travels around North America, answering the same questions with unflinching enthusiasm. We meet in the lobby of KPFA and neither of us needs much prep time. After introducing myself and congratulating him on another fine piece of work, I add, "I'm going to work you rather hard." And I explain about our tiny new radio station now beginning in West Marin. "Think of it like BBC Wales."

"Oh, not Wales, my dear. Please, not Wales." And we laugh our way into the recording studio.

It is an easy conversation and, as always, his enthusiasm for his life's work overflows into his charm, which allows his knowledge to fall gently from him to his audience. After reading the book, even as we talk, I learn more. Blackberry vines, Rubus rosaceae, can grow an inch a day. Fireweed, Chamaenerion angustifolium, is so called as it is the first plant to emerge from the forest floor after a fire, a bright and soothing balm for the regrowth of a forest. Little we knew that day how that tiny piece of knowledge would bring hope and comfort to the residents of Inverness, West Marin, and beyond. The conversation was a delight and remains a joyous memory for me, even as I accept that for Sir David, I was just one more appointment done and dusted.

I return home to the farm with two reels of quarter-inch audio tape and backup cassettes in my bag. As the family grew up and away, their rooms have changed from theirs to guest to office. I've taken over two. One for the editing tape machine and mixing board, and another for writing and office work. It is a busy and productive time, for I am home alone with a deadline of work to do. I treasure days like this. Some tough challenges are behind me and, though I see a few are ahead, I am not obsessively apprehensive. Not even too concerned about a conversation with our son a couple of weeks past.

We meet up in Berkeley, a coffee catch-up moment before each heading back into our lives. But Walter TY does have something on his mind.

"You remember those auditory hallucinations I had at college?"

I nod absently.

"Well, they've returned."

"Maybe it is time to get that looked at again."

"Maybe. But I'm off to climb the Grand Tetons with Mike. I'll check in when I get back."

"Okay." And we part.

Sir David is coming along nicely. A solid half hour for *Cover to Cover* at KPFA and then another hour to play for West Marin Community Radio. Even then, we called the station by that name. From its dusty beginnings in a broom cupboard of the Old Red Barn in Point Reyes, we had now moved to the 4H office above the barn space and were broadcasting on the Horizon Cable TV channel. It was new territory and exciting for this small band of radio-head enthusiasts as we began siting antennas, applying for the FCC license, and jumping those technical and bureaucratic hurdles that emerged before us.

And then October 1995 and the fires came, and so did my interview on West Marin Community Radio with Sir David. The Mount Vision Fire, traced to an unextinguished campfire on Inverness Ridge, burned deeply into the Point Reyes National Seashore. It blazed through 12,354 acres of parkland and destroyed forty-five Inverness homes that were nestled in the forest on the ridge. Probably not too many people tuned in to the little cable radio station, but some did and so the station began, with education and news in the face of disaster, becoming a part of this broader community.

★ ★ ★

It took a long time, days, to pry open the drawer of the memory box and find how I heard that Walter TY had had a grand mal seizure and was now in the emergency room at Kaiser Oakland Hospital. I needed to get there fast. I arrived to see his old Bolinas school friend, Jan Charlie Sears, now a paramedic, comfortingly at his side. Jan's presence was infinitely more reassuring to Walter than mine.

Another ambulance ride, now down to Redwood City and Kaiser Permanente Hospital with its specialty in neuroscience and neurosurgery. There are tests, the day spent in a fog before the late afternoon when Dr. Cecil Jun slips into the room and stands by Walter's bedside. Dr. Jun is a quiet man, neat and compact and as controlled in affect as one could wish. He addresses Walter more than me, with an old-world courtesy we are both grateful for. My friend Carolyn Brown has instinctively driven down to be with us. Dr. Jun speaks softly and clearly.

"There is a tumor in the right temporal lobe of your brain, and it needs to come out. You will, of course, want a second opinion."

In one sentence, he gives us news that changes a life forever, before the courtesy of returning the control of that life, for the moment.

It has taken three days to get this far and then phone Rome, speaking first to Walter's assistant, Danny Farrell, telling him of this news and that I would be telling Walter.

Ten days later, we are together as parents in the surgical waiting room at Kaiser Permanente. The hospital is still a strange and unfamiliar place for us, but one we would come to know well, as it, and our visits there, continue to expand over the years. While waiting, pacing, and fearing everything we imagined, my phone rings. It is Ewan MacDonald from town. An old friend has just pitched up, dockside, on his doorstep. David Grant, his wife Kate, their three children, Eilidh (Ali), Torcuil, and Fionn. They have arrived in a horse-drawn caravan with a large farm hound and draft horse, Traceur, and have journeyed from Japan by way of Los Angeles as they travel around the world. Starting in Holland, it would take them seven years to eventually make it back to Scotland. Ewan was now tasked with finding them a place to rest up for much of the winter. Hence the midday phone call,

Could we take the horse, Traceur, for them?

Of course we did. Traceur would become a gentle part of the full, intensely interesting winter months ahead: having a horse back on the farm; Walter TY recovering from his brain surgery; deciding on his next treatment options; the hayloft becoming an editing suite for *The English Patient*; the FedEx delivery man arriving daily with video cassettes from footage that has been filmed in Tunisia, transferred from film to tape in Rome, and coded and set up in Bolinas. Weeks later, the production team returned from Italy and everyday, a carload with an assortment of producers, writer Michael Ondaatje and director Anthony Minghella, arrived at the farm for lunch before gathering to sit on the library floor, tea and biscuits in hand, looking at footage still coming in. As everyone got settled into this new routine, I noticed the truck was missing, and so was Gene, the gardening help. Both needed to be found, but this was not quite the moment.

During a last check-in before Walter TY was released from the hospital, Dr. Jun guided us to the post-surgical care of Irene Brown, a Scottish nurse, as short as I am tall, who became a beloved friend. He ended our conversation, "I'm so sorry. Good luck." Not every surgeon looks beyond the operating suite or his office to the lives that might unfold beyond his intervention. When at a later date we asked him what it was like to remove a burst tumor, he replied, "Gently scooping as much cream of wheat as you can from a bowl of oatmeal."

With a choice of five different pathology readings and diagnoses of the tumor cells, Walter TY rejected both radiation and chemotherapy. This proved to be the right decision as, in those days, both therapies were prescribed with a heavy hand and, for a few years, often caused more damage than relief.

Epilepsy had arrived, entering our lives like an unwanted yet determined houseguest. Walter TY continues to ride these waves with all the courage and fortitude he can muster. Electric pulses beat along with blood through his brain as he works to balance meaning and safety along his life's journey. New treatments are tried, but to this day, medication is only partially successful in holding his continued seizures at bay. His dreams of teaching wilderness skills and lead mountaineering expeditions, taking a path away from the influences of his family, must dissolve. Though those physical mountains remain in the distance for him, he continues to teach us all many of life's lessons. His father gathered him to his work; TY has the sense of balance and rhythm needed by a good film editor. As an editorial assistant, he is a patient and kind man to have by your side, resourceful when schedules, film, and people overflow into chaos.

The blessings of a small town for a family in acute crisis always include food. Shopping was done and meals were brought by, while everyone knew everything there was to know, which, for several years, brought phone calls and knocks on the door. "We have a brain tumor too." As always, it is in the sharing of these stories that comfort comes.

Eventually, things calmed down. The film crew decamped to Berkeley. We found and recovered the truck from a wrecking yard in Richmond, and Traceur settled into a well-earned rest, enjoying the fresh winter grass that was just emerging. I could again take comfort in my barn chores, which included feeding Traceur extra hay, added to his field grazing.

★ ★ ★

In the early-morning winter light I would see Ali curled up on the hay bales, awake and reading by the time I walked through the barn. We didn't talk much. A buried memory told me she needed space and quiet, a place for her mind and body to rest, heal from travel, and grow. Children are amazingly resilient, moving through the thoughtless obstacles we put in their way, and Ali was strong. Both Ali and her brother Torcuil found mentors in Bolinas. Jason Wonders took Ali onto his endurance riding team, while Keith Hansen opened the doors into the world of ornithology for Torcuil. Those winter months created a place for these two to find the seeds they could nurture and grow into their adult worlds. It was a deep rest, one this geography can give, and one the family needed before carrying on, traveling north and east across America before eventually making it home to Scotland.

So why was that so hard? What did I see when I looked at Ali curled up on the hay bales in our barn? Something I recognized completely but had put away in the memory box of betrayal. Something Dorothy tries to accept in all her *Oz* adventures. That adults, even those with the best of intentions, are not always to be trusted. And when, as a child, you find that out, there is a shock, and you are startled and afraid. And you must find your own courage.

Do animals feel that, yearling colts when they are moved out of the herd to make way for the next generation? Children do, when adults teach one way of being and then demand the opposite for their own reasons, breaking their belief in the certainty of their world. It was such a breach at St. Catherine's school that led me to leave. Instilled, via our housemistress, with the code of *you sink and swim together*, and then to have it turned on its head as she tried to make me betray my friends when the staff wanted information. I walked.

I closed the door of my housemistress's tiny bed-sitting room and without thinking, left the central old school building and found my way onto the small village railway station next to the school grounds, taking the train and a bus as far as my two-shillings pocket money would go, to the Aldershot rail station, and then to walk some more. I knew my way, five miles across country. Home, but not home. To the farm, behind the old stone farmhouse, beside the open fields, where a huge corrugated metal barn had been built sometime in my lifetime as I can remember it being "new." It was summer and I was warm enough in my cotton blue-checked uniform dress and navy cardigan. As dusk came, the cowman's son, Dave, finished with the afternoon milking and walking home for his tea, saw me. Did we speak? I don't remember. I climbed to the top of the twenty-bale haystack and nestled in to sleep. Before dawn broke, Dave's silhouette was just outlined as he walked into the barn on his way to early-morning milking. He wasn't sure I would still be there, but he had stolen biscuits in his pocket, just in case. Dave kept my secret all that day and through the following night. But during the next day when I climbed down to stretch my legs, gather warmth from the summer sun, and steal a mug of milk from the cowshed, Dave's father, Bill the cowman, and the older farmhands saw me and began to talk among themselves. No one had yet come to the farm to look for me, but they must have known it would happen. The next morning, Dave brought more biscuits and I ate those too. I have no memory of hunger, discomfort, only an overwhelming sense that if I could just stay there, I would be safe. Within the hay barn's warm, embracing cave, I was not afraid. But by teatime of the second full day, the men came to the barn. They gathered around the base of the stacked hay, softly calling me down from the high bales as if coaxing a creature out of its den.

"You have to go home now. Your mother is worried about you."

I couldn't imagine that. But they were firm and I understood that without their support, the barn would no longer be my safe haven. Norman was the one to walk with me to the crest of the Station Bridge. Pushing his bike beside us, he talked gently, assuring me it would be all right; they, whoever they were, would be so relieved I was safe that no one would be angry with me. For two years in devoted puppy love I had followed Norman and learned from him the safety of gentle, loving kindness within the rhythm of the seasons unfolding. No one else could have led me back into the world in which I must live. We walked the length of the Cove Road, turned into the last stretch to crest at the Station Bridge, and stopped.

"Here you are. You can cross the road and walk home now. It's only a little ways." He stayed on the station side of the road and watched as I crossed the bridge and down the slope onto Elvetham Road. It had not yet been a year since my father had died, my mother had sold our home and moved closer into the small town to begin a new life. I didn't look back as I walked alone along the street to her new home.

Chapter 11

Apple Harvest

The end of October, it is autumn on the farm and in my years, and finally, here is the harvest I have been working for, the gathering of apples and cider pressing. John Perry from Stinson Beach moved from Pony Club father supreme to apple cider presser-in-chief when he trucked over the apple press he had made from cherrywood felled and milled from his wife Beth's family farm in Minnesota. John was happy to see the press come to life again in a new home and carefully instructed me as to its particular intricacies, though for the first couple of years, he would always set it up and run it himself. Then after an hour or so, as people came to the farm with their own apples to press, he and a chum or two would rest up—watching, mind you—while leaning on the sides of their flatbed trucks parked close by in the field, to sample the Black Jack that was their version of hard cider. Over the years, community apple pressing at our farm and others' became an annual event, as families from town and West Marin brought crates and bags of apples, along with empty jars to fill with their juice. During those first years I felt like a little red hen, watched by my very dubious and curious house roosters. But when in six months came the first taste-testing time, there was some grudging respect as glasses were refilled around the table.

The thrice-moved trees had begun to sort themselves out. Some faded with hardly an effort, flat out refusing to take root and grow with my scandalous neglect. Others struggled to find a footing, and some just settled in and reached down. Slowly, I added a chosen tree or two each year, then some home-grafted trees that leapt at the chance to take root and flourish. More grafted apple trees are growing; the varieties are chosen for willingness to grow with us, rescued scion from old trees as well as for flavor and use. Over the years we learned by taste, if not by science, of the richness or lack of the flavor and health in the apples we pressed and the juice and cider we made. We learned how to do it.

Mum's Tips for Harvest and Pressing:

A week or a few days before pressing:

1. Pick apples and keep varieties separated and in boxes in the shed so you can see what the mix looks like. The apples will sweat and sweeten while they wait.

2. Check that you have the right stoppers and corks for containers.

3. Bring out, check over, and repeatedly hose down and soak the press to relax and swell the wood. This is boat work.

The night before or the early morning the day of your press:

4. Wash out everything—glass containers, stoppers, buckets, and bathtub—with a mild bleach rinse, and rinse again.

5.   Scratch out a drainage ditch from the old bathtub by the fence line.

6.   Clean off the shelf in the old metal horse stall where you will put the filled jugs. The main thing is to have everything super-clean, but not deadly sterile.

7.   Hold back some big mason jars for and of juice. You will want some juice for drinking, now and at Thanksgiving, and also for topping up the big fermenting jars as the cider begins to bubble.

Every family and farm will make cider according to the persuasion of its press. Suffice to say that the old press made by John Perry makes far superior mush and juice than the little dinky "fun" press for small batches.

8.   When the press is over, clean everything off really well, dry, and sun clean before putting all the equipment away.

Have fun and take pictures.

The apple press is over and the two glass carboys are corked with twelve gallons of apple juice. It is exciting to see the movement as the juice turns and rises up and through the stoppers. This afternoon, the sky was full of rain. Now that the apple press is done, I think it would be good to take the Walterses into the orchard and show them where this harvest actually came from. I gave them each a pair of clippers in case there was a little tidying to do, and we set out. From the back of the orchard, I proudly showed them this year's eleven new grafted young trees. Even with the trees now almost all bare of fruit, it looked so lovely. Walter TY was walking along two rows with intent and then he called, "Mum, look at Dad." His father stood where we had left him, at the top of the orchard. Clippers in hand, he was looking up at the moon, now visible as dusk was sliding into night. His mind was somewhere, above and beyond the trees and us all.

The Indian summer blast of heat is over, no longer sweetening the last of the apples hanging on the trees or filling the winter squash with rich pulp. The sun is still shining brightly but now carries only a winter warmth. A faint clip, not yet a nip, but just a dip in the temperature tells the fruit there will be no more help from the sun this year. The pear, medlar, apple, and persimmon tree leaves are turning color from green to orange and brown, signs that their summer harvest is over. In the orchard, the two Pippin apple trees, one a Cox's, the other a Hauer, are tucked away in a microclimate pocket, sheltered by the farmhouse and the rows of eucalyptus trees around the back. They are the only trees whose leaves are still green. I gathered a few windfalls but left some fruit on the Cox's Orange Pippin tree, saving them for eating apples. A few apples were well hidden by dull green foliage on the tree. They won't be ready until the end of November or even the beginning of December. This was my father's favorite apple from his orchard in England. I grow it for him, though I'm not sure how much the Cox's really likes California. Truthfully, the Hauer Pippin seems happiest and, grudgingly, I have come to accept that.

Later in the week, I went to gather some more Cox's but there was not an apple to be found! Who comes into the orchard? Coyote, raccoon, fox, or possum? All have climbed and shaken the trees to eat their fill of the still-unripe fruit. I have a small basket left, now stored on racks in the shed. Now we need to be vigilant again and keep the stored harvest from the rats! But am grateful for the apples' taste of memory and childhood and my father's early-morning tea tray.

A murder of crows has reached a new density that is visible throughout the farm. Or, to put it another way, the arable farming has reached a density to affect the crows. Mickey was wondering what was eating the brassica leaves. It turns out to be the crows. They are now onto the apples that are not yet ripe. As we begin to harvest the pears in September, the crows join us. They start and stay in the topmost branches, taking out all the pears we cannot and dare not reach.

Over the weekend, Annabelle Lenderink, who manages Star Route Farms, set out a row of red and silver sparkles alongside half of the fenceline across the road. They twinkle and blink ferociously and light up the cars across the lagoon. She made, and installed, a scarecrow who looks just like Worzel Gummidge from the English children's book of long ago. His arms are outstretched, waving in the breeze. His straw hat looks jaunty and worn.

On Tuesday the crows were all sitting lined up on the fence posts, looking towards the field at Annabelle's scarecrow and the glitter dangling. By Thursday they have decided to ignore the glitter and the scarecrow and dive back into the field. They are not yet sitting on the scarecrow. Next door on the Franklin farm Vickisa has better luck, hanging CDs on the plum tree. Maybe we can try that too.

Best Beets

"Bolinas grows the Best Beets," said Peter Martinelli at an autumnal luncheon held at his farm by MALT (Marin Agricultural Land Trust), and Peter should know. He is quoting from his own experience and also from *The History of Marin County*, California written by J.P. Munroe-Fraser, who noted the same in 1880.

Peter Martinelli is a hard-working farmer who carries old knowledge beside courtly wisdom, both varieties of the same species of goodness and commonsense. Peter also carries the farming gene. While not directly related to S. Martinelli Sparkling Apple Company, one could follow and find faint connections via those curlicue links that loosely connect families sharing the same name. When his grandparents, Joran and Genevieve Martinelli, purchased 360 acres tucked into and over a hillside in Bolinas, the families spent their summers there enjoying Paradise Valley, along with all its seasonal glory. During Peter's childhood he grew (how could one not) to love the land and with his father, each summer, would grow a vegetable garden. Seeds were planted, not only in the summer gardens they grew, but deep in Peter's heart. But with a fourth-generational family lineage of Marin County lawyers, Peter's path was cut out for him in East Marin and he duly graduated from UC Berkeley Law School. It took a family blessing, and no doubt a sigh, before Peter was able to return to the land.

"Leaving academic pursuits behind, I went to work for Warren Weber in the mid-1980s," Peter said when I checked in with him. It must have been an amazing time, as together the young local farmers learned the ways of the land and what it was ready to yield. Beginning with just a quarter of an acre in the 1990s as one of the first truly organic commercial farmers in the Northern Bay Area Counties, Peter is, for now, the one of the family destined to continue to farm the Martinelli Family Ranch. The main agricultural component of the farm is the approximately twenty-two acres of Fresh Run Farms, though Peter's sister-in-law Susan has produced stunning jams, jellies, eggs, and wool that all carry her mark.

Peter's beetroot was one of the early success stories of organic farming in this area. In the 1980s, the early days of farmers markets, Peter could be found standing at his truck, smiling and laughing, unloading crates holding bunches of big red beetroots and shiny bunches of chard. As fast as he unloaded the crates, the bunches were snatched into baskets and scuttled off to restaurant and home kitchens.

Almost all our arable farmers grow great beets. Warren, Peter, Dennis, and Mickey. Even we grow good beets! They are a steady staple, growing and harvested almost all year round. The farmstands and farmers markets are hardly ever without at least one box of beets. Beetroot has long ago been elevated to a super-good-for-you vegetable. The beet greens, along with the dark crimson roots cut into bite-sized sections, are tossed in with paint-white feta cheese on a salad. The leaves are big and bushy, making sweeter vegetable juices than the ever-prescribed kale, which is good, or curly-kale, which, like a peroxided hard workin' gal, can be bitter or bland.

Detroit Dark Red is the old favorite beetroot staple to grow. Dependable and sturdy, yet delicate and sweet. But Mickey and some of the other farmers branched out, for customer demand and higher prices, into golden-yellow and striped varieties. With a steady supply of water (something ours don't always get), beets grow fast. But they must not have too much water, or the bulbs get big, difficult to handle, and lose their delicate flavor. Beets are resilient and the little worms that can wreak havoc with carrots don't have time or energy to take on the hardy red beetroot.

When summer gives way to autumn, the dark beets lie subdued beside the bold orange winter squash bursting with fresh-grown pride. The spring greens that were bright and brave in the fields now take on a more somber hue.

And what happened to borscht, good old beetroot soup? Green watercress and sorrel soups brighten our bowls in spring, while the creamy yellow Hubbard and butternut squashes have taken over the autumn and winter menus. Borscht comes from Ukraine, and Ievgen Klopotenko, an internationally renowned chef from Lviv, is cooking borscht to unite his war-torn country and reclaim the heritage of this dish for the Ukraine. Like many restaurants struggling to hold on during the war with Russia, his kitchen now serves both his regular and international diners, along with cooking hundreds of meals for refugees. While there are borscht recipes from Ukraine, Eastern Europe, and Russia, each of them adding various potatoes, vegetables, and meats, Ukraine claims to be the home of this humble yet hearty soup.

My recipe was birthed from *Gourmet Cook Book Volume Two*, an early-1969, probably desperate (my cooking was still a hit-and-miss affair) Christmas gift from my husband. But it has been long since tweaked and fiddled with.

A simple borscht recipe to use wherever you are:

Yields about 4 servings.

- 4 red beets

- 2 carrots

- 1 onion

- Fresh bay leaves, sage, thyme, and chives from the garden.

- Olive oil, salt, pepper, caraway, and cumin from the cupboard.

- I mason jar (4 cups) chicken or vegetable stock from the freezer.

1. Parboil the beets in their skins until a knife slips in easily.

2. Lift the beets into a bowl to cool before you skin them.

3. Strain and save the beet water. Some recipes call for throwing out the water, which is ridiculous, though it does need straining to remove any leftover farm soil and grit.

4. While the beets are cooling, heat the olive oil in a big saucepan.

5. Add the chopped onions to sweat slowly as you peel and slice the carrots.

6. When the onion is softened to a sweet yellow add the chopped carrots and then the caraway and cumin to taste. I use a fair bit of both spices.

7. Stir for a while until the carrots are glistening.

8. Any wine in the fridge? A glug can go in now.

9. Stir some more and then add the thyme, bay leaves (at least 2), and sprig of sage. Salt and pepper now if you like.

10. When you feel the flavors have been properly introduced then pour in the stock.

11. Bring to a simmer and cook until the carrots are soft.

12. Time to slip the skins off the beetroots, give them a rough chop, and add to the mix.

13. Do you need to add more liquid? If so, you have the beet water on hand. Add as necessary.

14. When this is all cooked up nicely, twenty minutes or so, turn off the heat. Put on the saucepan lid and go and do something else for at least an hour.

15. Only then, come back and fish out the bay leaves, thyme stalk, and sprig of sage.

16. Blend the soup until there are no lumps. How does it feel? How does it taste? I like a firmish consistency and to be able to taste the caraway with a hint of cumin. Adjust the liquid with more beet water and flavor with seasoning. The soup is ready now, but will be better still after sitting a little longer.

Maybe because borscht is from Eastern Europe, most recipes call for potatoes rather than carrots, and a thick Greek yogurt. But this soup was made in London, using a dollop of fresh Devonshire cream before sprinkling on the chopped chives from the garden.

And the little glass of wine? Well, I didn't put all of it in the soup—just a glug, not two.

And Peter's Strawberries

While I was researching something or other, Peter lent me his copy of *The History of Marin County*. Written by J. P. Munroe-Fraser, it was first published in 1880 and holds an in-depth, well-researched account of the social geography of early Marin and how Marin County developed around agriculture. In the 1880s, all farm trails led to Nicasio, which was then the geographic center hub of Marin and slated to be the county seat. It was only when other industries and modes of transport moved into the county that the seat was changed to San Rafael.

I loved Peter's book. The geography of the land seemed to draw the same crazy characters to outlying towns such as ours and the other West Marin hamlets, as it does today. Back when other Europeans were jostling and jousting with the Spanish, who had almost swept the area clear of Coast Miwok native tribes, the hometown laws of the Old West and new American settlements were more efficient than most county courts.

At this time in our lives, it would be close to eleven p.m. when my husband returned from work in Lucas Valley. He would sit in his chair, sipping from a mug of Green & Blacks Hot Chocolate, laced with a solid shot of Jameson Irish Whiskey, and close his eyes while I read aloud to him from Peter's book. Asleep, I often thought. The book was so fragile that the spine fell away with use, so I had carefully wrapped it in brown-bag paper such as we used to do in boarding school to help hold old textbooks together. A month or so passed before I realized it was time to return the book to Peter, but suddenly it was AWOL. Was it possible that my husband had taken it to work? It certainly was, and he had been reading from it to his post-production crew at lunchtime, following the passages I had read to him the previous evening! On a lunch-time date, often the only real way we had of visiting with each other, I eased it from the stable yard office, wondering why there was so little fuss. The answer came a few days later, via Amazon, when a newly printed version—reissued in 1972—of our own arrived in the mail.

But there was still the challenge of returning Peter's copy to him. The days I searched for him on his farm, he was at market. I went to the local Saturday market, but that day, he was off at the city farmers market. We messaged, as one does with anyone under forty, and I was instructed to leave the book on the boot-bench outside our back porch, where it sat for days. Peter's goats had escaped and scampered into the next-door family's garden. Naughty, happy goats. More days passed until, after walking back through the afternoon sunlight in the barn from adding more greens to the compost bin, I saw that the book was gone. There, in its place, was a box of Pete's finest strawberries. I sat down beside them, intrigued by the sight and the smell. Mitzi joined me. The heart-shaped fruit shone out of the little baskets sitting snugly together in the box and smelled of strawberries. They looked and tasted of strawberries. I raised one berry to my face, closed my eyes, and fell into memories of my childhood home in England, basket in hand, climbing under the cage-netting, releasing the small birds caught there before plucking and eating forever strawberries. Farmer friends share the best gifts, ever. Thank you, Peter.

A note here: Strawberries and cream, strawberries and meringue, strawberries and honey, but never, never ruin real (Peter's) good strawberries with chocolate. Never, ever.

Paradise Valley

Andrew was a new young farmer raising water buffalo in Point Reyes, and on Saturday I went to the Point Reyes Farmers Market specifically looking for his mozzarella cheese. And eggplants. Got the cheese and other things-I-was-not-looking-to-buy, and could not help but buy beets and lettuce from the Dierks, Sandy and Dennis, who always make a fantastic presentation of their really good produce. The displays unfold like one of Sandy's quilts that she fashions with fabric, often from Guatemala. Sandy has been a quiet gatherer of the quilting community in town. Each year, Sandy's quilts would be on display at Toby's Feed Barn, the local community center, or museum before being auctioned off for that year's charity. And every year, I look at the quilts with admiration and awe. They are all so beautiful, a far cry from the first and only project I ventured into, when three of us West Marin midwifes came together to make a baby quilt for the fourth, who was pregnant. But today I was admiring their vegetables. Into my basket went a big bunch of beets that did not look—nor were they upon tasting—bolted or old. They had a fine, sweet flavor. The lettuce was tightly packed in pans, like bouquets of flowers, and I chose one each of three different varieties. I have no idea what they were, but they looked beautiful and tasted great. We don't think of lettuce as having a taste, but it does.

When it came time to wash the lettuce and slice away at the base, I had to cut deep; the lettuces, each one, were tightly bound and grown. How so? Water restricted? I don't think so. Speed—slow or fast? What makes them different? There were none of those loose-leafed and over-watered ones, rushed through their seventy-five to eighty growing days.

On Fridays, Star Route Farms sets out a farmstand by their roadside field. The vegetables are harvested from far back in the fields while the parsley and chervil is cut and bunched as a chef cuts—that is, short-stemmed and bound tight, ready for a quick rinse before chopping from the bunch.

Gospel Flat Farms

The Gospel Flat Farms stand is now a town destination, drawing out-of-towners (a funny phrase) who know they can come to Bolinas for farm-fresh vegetables and crabs when in season. In the mid-1960s and '70s, The Gibson House and Tarantino restaurants were Bolinas destinations for serious food lovers and inspirations for the next generation of chefs. Now Mickey's Farm Stand has become the place of harvest, for food and community, albeit in a commercial sense, where people gather as they stop on their way in or out of town. We come by bicycle, car, or Shank's pony to buy our food. The cars range from clapped-out old trucks of ancient lineage, dusty with-it Subarus, and very shiny—under their dust—BMWs. At least half of the cars are loaded with surfboards. On the weekends, the farmstand is as good a place as any to see the changing faces of our town. These years are bringing another seismic shift in population, just as it was when we came to town in the 1960s and '70s, each wave of people pushing on the preceding wave and sending it, or us, hurtling into the sand.

Don Murch of Gospel Flat Farms loves to fish and for many years now has gone north to Alaska, fishing several seasons in a row with a northern fisherman / farmer buddy who happens to grow turnips. It took years for the friendship to become strong enough to the point that an Alaskan would part with his home-grown seed. Don brought the seed south and planted it. It grows very well and Don's Alaskan turnips are the sweetest, whitest turnips I've ever tasted.

Fishermen

In 2014, when I left to join Walter on location in Vancouver for Brad Bird's *Tomorrowland*, the second (Disney) film Walter was fired from, all of Don's crab pots were lined up along the farm driveway with the buoys freshly painted orange and white. When does a fisherman, never mind a farmer, have time to do those chores, especially as the California weather keeps you outdoors and busy all year round?

The weather forecast keeps pushing the rain to tomorrow, and tomorrow. The sky certainly looks full of moisture, and the air feels it too. But there is a wind blowing across the mountain and into the channel that is argumentative, querulous, and sullen—all at the same time.

This year, the commercial crab season opens on November 15, and days before that date, the pots were resting on the wharf quayside, ready and waiting to go back in the ocean. As we take our beach walks, all the town is watching the pots, and anticipation of the crab season is growing. Apparently, it got off to a good start. The crabs are healthy and robust. We, like most of us here, will enjoy some crabs over the Thanksgiving holiday weekend.

Fishing used to be a viable livelihood for several full-time fishermen in town, but the channel silting in along with the county, and the coastal governments adding their chokehold regulations here and there—without always taking in all the seafaring knowledge here—has made it hard for those who are still holding on. Josh Churchman has wrestled with the sea and the bureaucracy for years, and the sea remains his honored friend. He has captured his stories, memories, and miracles in *The Whale That Lit the World*.

Our commercial fishermen are strong. Jeremy Dierks is no longer a boy-wonder fisherman, but a grown man who long ago joined the ranks of Josh Churchman and his son, Robbie Knowles of the Pepper family, and Don and Mickey Murch. Chuck Oakander's son, Reid, helps Alby from the gas station prepare and lay out his pots. The pots are big and cumbersome. This is a young man's game. They are much too heavy for Alby Foreman now, but he loves to go crabbing. Alby complains to Chuck, and anyone else who will listen, about his body giving out on him.

Jeremy strides into the café's back entrance with two crates of live crabs. Robbie and Josh also sell their crabs in and out of town. Don has his sign out at the road farmstand: *Live Crab 4-6 p.m. Friday, Saturday, and Sunday.*

Ewan MacDonald gave us two cooked crabs to welcome us back from Vancouver. The recreational season begins earlier and lasts longer than the commercial. The crabs looked good, strong, and healthy, and fat adults are abundant. How many can you catch in a basket at one time when you pull them up from the seabed?

This is party time and here is our version (with her blessing) of the sublime

Peggy Knickerbocker's Crab Dinner, from her book *Simple Soirées*:

Use one crab per person for four people; thereafter, cut one away, unless your diners are all male and under fifty years old. In which case, they will eat the lot.

1. Crush 6 cloves of garlic.

2. Roughly chop one full bunch of Italian parsley.

3. Two teaspoons of red pepper flakes.

4. Good grind of black pepper.

5. A cup of fine olive oil.

6. Juice of at least two Meyer lemons.

7. With two people at the kitchen sink, clean the freshly cooked crab. Drain the meat as it comes free.

8. In a large bowl, mix the cracked crab and the marinade. Add more olive oil and lemon juice as necessary—to taste, as they say—but not really because the marinade will change its flavor as it matures. Place this big bowl in the fridge.

9. Open the wine.

10. Lay the table. Include crab crackers. Large old-fashioned soup bowls are better than plates.

11. Add finger bowls with lemon wedges. Make sure there are good table napkins for everyone.

12. If not done already, prepare a cheese board with fresh fruit for dessert.

13. Make a lovely crisp lettuce salad. Nothing too fancy here, you really want just bright lettuce, maybe some chives and pomegranate seeds, but don't add too much.

14. Fresh baguettes. If I have had the time, I will make it.

15. Light the candles.

16. Transfer the crab and marinade to a lovely serving bowl and place it on the table.

17. Bring the salad, bread, olive oil, salt and pepper, the wine, and water.

Take a moment of thanksgiving. I can see it all now...

Chapter 12

Winter Watching

On Monday, there was just a single robin, but now there is a sizable flock. I am still surprised at the size of the American robin compared to the dainty robin redbreast of England. Today they are back, drinking from a knothole in the pear tree that formed after we cut off a cracked branch. When limbs have been severed, the stub shrinks in on itself, as if understanding that as one purpose has been removed with the limb, now another must be found and so the wood shrivels and implodes, making a hollow to catch what moisture it can. From the living room window, I watched one robin as he dipped his bill to the hollow and raised it again to swallow the water. From where has this flock returned? And how long do they stay? Long enough to breed here. This happy flock has claimed the trees along the roadside in front of the farm.

There continues to be an early frost that disappears the moment the sun looks at the grass. It is cold enough for the rhubarb to wilt and go dormant; for the sap to stay low, retreat from rising in the fruit trees. This is all good. As the Walterses and I came back from Ron and Jill's Christmas houseboat clan gathering in Mill Valley, the boys let me off at the Gospel Flat Farms stand. I bought some parsley and then walked home. So organically has the farmstand grown that it looks like it has always been there. We welcome its presence and each new addition it brings, as much as we do a new flower or vegetable in our own garden. Someone was out on the red rooster cart and we waved a greeting. Last night, a tree came down behind the farm stand. Two chainsaws are resting there after being worked hard, beginning to clear the wood. But now the spot behind the stand is clear. It will give rise to some chin / beard-stroking and pondering.

The weather patterns are no longer predictable, and it feels as if real change is in the atmosphere all around us. As if a storm is coming. But a storm of what, and from where? This is the driest winter it has been for years as recorded by Ralph Camiccia, who puts out his weekly rain and precipitation report every week in the *Hearsay News*. Ralph took over from Jack Siedman, who took over from fire chief Jose Silva, who sent daily reports to the Army Corps of Engineers for their flood-control network. The Army Corps no longer requires reports and drought floods are not the concern of these years. The Bolinas Community Public Utility District (BCPUD) is already sending out mailings, asking us all to be careful with our water usage. The governor of California, Jerry Brown, is about to call California a drought state of emergency. We all read Ralph's reports, putting numbers on a page in the *Hearsay News* and comparing them and us to previous years.

But sometimes there is hope and, like today, the sky is finally raining, steadily in a workmanlike manner. No gusty show-off winds, no fainthearted flurries followed by a motionless pout, just rain, filling the water barrels to overflowing and sounding a fast staccato drip-drip from an overhang onto the deck. There is enough rain to have it slide toward the concrete lip into the barn and then turn to the trench and into the field beyond. It didn't come through the skylight in the bathroom, which says the storm is not mildly torrential, and I am thankful.

Mickey Murch drove in from Gospel Flat Farms. Suddenly he is grown up, farming fast and hard with the energy of a young family farming man. He is scouring the community for land and feeding the community at his Gospel Flat Farms stand. More than a breath of fresh air, he is a whirlwind of energy. Now he is farming two of our fields and today came by to drop off loads of manure for the apple trees. It is good to have another, younger, more energetic and determined farmer around. Our beautiful river-bottom soil fields, so well fed from the horses of old, are grateful for his attention and rise almost joyfully under his disking. But now that he has tilled the ground in the orchard, the soil is so soft that I can't get in using my own little tractor. Then suddenly, the soil is crusty on top while below it grows heavy, with the water table receding and pulling soil down with the moisture.

Mickey is wrapped up warmly: a big, old, red wooly hat squashing his hair and a fleece jacket that never claimed to support an old school or pro team. He is pulling some machine for either harrowing or disking, not yet planting.

The cold snap is giving us a breather. Later, I will try to spread more mulch on all the apple trees. For each tree, I use half a wheelbarrow of compost, a gallon of ash, and a cup of borax. There are bales of old alfalfa hay in the barn so I can add flakes of hay over the compost and manure. If it is to be another dry year, then the heavy mulch will help retain moisture even as it provides good nesting for the field mice! The pruning can wait until after feeding. If we do have more rain, I want the manure and compost on the ground.

Will, another young farmer from Gospel Flat Farms, drove over on the red hot-rod trailer. What are those called? The bright red body is a cheerful colour and the young farmers gun that baby up and down Gospel Flats like we used to gallop our horses along the roadside on our way to the beach, grabbing the time free from our children whenever we could. Will is built like Mickey, maybe with an added ten pounds but no more. He wears the same thick beard, which makes ladies of a certain age smile. He is dressed in the same style of wool, ear-muffed hat rammed down on his head. A black mountain bomber jacket, fatigue-green trousers, heavy socks, and boots. All the same as Mickey's, yet Will's posture and walk are heavier, as if he carries burdens and concerns deep in his heart and hidden under his jacket.

Will is harvesting crate after crate of sprouting broccoli. They sell it loose, straight from the crate. Maybe they give it a hose-over or maybe not, depending on the rain wash. I watch Will crouch, bend, cut, and toss as he moves along these two almost-spent rows. At the end of the row, there are two plants that got away and are blooming in pale, spring-yellow florets. Then Mickey will plow up his brassicas. Toss and chop them. Where the plough throws curves, the soil will look shiny and hard, drying out harshly under these winds. Mickey can then come through the apple tree rows to make it easier for me to walk in the orchard.

I'm watching Will because today is Friday, my farm day. It is raining and I cannot, must not, disturb the soil or prune. I am very grateful for when I felt strong enough to spread the mulch muck and add the wood ash to the apple trees. It is a wonderful feeling when you get something right like that. But now it is time to bottle the cider.

Apple Cider

Sean Thackrey is a world-renowned viniculturist. He is also Irish and thus a born lover of literature and the spoken word. He is a true Renaissance man, an artist of a particular rugged humor with a thirst for knowledge and curiosity for art that continually lead him forward into more winemaking. His knowledge and appreciation of beauty in all artistic and literate endeavors are legendary. The sun was shining and the air comfortable when, outside the post office, Sean and I talked between that midmorning moment, an errand and a chore, both leaning across the bed of his truck. He has heard of my beginnings at making apple cider, the real stuff, and he is heartened and very encouraging. Sean has—of course he does—old Middle English manuscripts, replete with directions on the growing, harvesting, and pressing of apples for cider, as well as its uses. He wanted to make copies of the manuscript to give to me and I eagerly accepted his offer. A few days later he showed up at the farm with a slim folder of pages. They are precious, for the information is not only simple and insightful but that Sean is reaching out and sharing his treasures and knowledge is just the best encouragement, a gift beyond price.

★ ★ ★

Instead of working in the orchard, today is apple cider bottling day. The six-gallon jars hold clear cider. Fermentation is over and the sediment has settled at the bottom of the jars. This year, maybe because of less water, the apples seemed tougher, with a higher level of tannic, and the cider in the bell jars stayed cloudy. In November I added a glug-glug of our home honey to the pure apple juice. That is it.

The system is simple. There is just work to be done. I must bring the bottles in from the shed to the kitchen. Turn the oven on to 200 degrees. Wash the bottles in mild soapy water and rinse. Stack them in the oven for just a few minutes until they are dryish. There is a lot of clinking and clashing as I ram bottles into the oven, trying to fit in as many as I can and getting this boring bit done quickly. I'm trying not to track too much mud into the kitchen, but this chore is a bit wet and sloppy, though truthfully, I've reached an age where I don't really care too much if I make a mess. This is why we have always had painted wood floors and a rug that hides almost every indiscretion. So I can mop. The most important thing in the process is to be clean—clean more than sterile, though maybe I shouldn't say that. But sterility in the process deadens the cider, literally. I make a new label every year and really should begin to ask what is needed to produce apple cider commercially.

The rain is still coming down steadily and the first early pink plum blossom is falling on the plywood bench and beehive I left sitting outside the shed. I bring the little orange crate that will serve as my bottling table into the shed, but don't brush off the fallen blossoms. They sparkle and still long to be alive.

Now the bottles are standing upright on the baking tray, balanced precariously on the orange crate. I unstop the first jar. In goes the hose (that I washed along with the bottles in the kitchen) and I suck, drawing the cider into the tube. It rushes willingly into the waiting bottles. I must be quick to keep up, moving the tubing from bottle to bottle, wasting as little cider as possible. The cider still sits in my mouth until, finally, I swallow and realize this batch is really good. The process is repeated, bottle after bottle, until all the bottles on the tray are filled. I lift out the tubing—gently, so as not to disturb the sediment—and fold it back into the jar to rest. Carefully, I carry the tray with a dozen bottles into the shed for capping.

Then I start again. Each start required another suck and pull on the tubing, and by morning's end I have drunk a good half pint of cider, which has gone down a treat. It is just perfect. Methodically I go on until nine to eleven gallons of cider are stored and capped and sit waiting for this year's label. Time to clear things away. I wipe off the counter to keep the wood rats, who have obviously been helping themselves to the cider over-flow, sober.

As I finish with the cider, Will pulls out of the field, closing the gate behind him, and spins fresh mud from his tires onto the driveway. I pulled in an old beehive from the orchard field, cleaned it up, and gave it a good coat of paint. As soon as it dries, it will be ready to go out again.

The plum tree dips and bows under the weight of the rain-held blossoms; some fall, some wait, not yet open. Up on the hill, hidden behind and beneath scrub willow, two more plum trees bloom. One is white; one is pink. Each year, they hold on. I wonder who planted them. Are they the remains of a long-for-gotten family orchard or the project of a secret cache buried and forgotten by frugal scrub jays?

Blue Heron Breakfast

Now that the early rains have arrived, the soil is quickly becoming soft and the gophers are moving easily through it. There is a lot of work for them to do. They will clean the fallen dirt from their underground burrows just as above ground, farmers will clear those tree limbs brought down in the first autumn's wind and rainstorms. The week after the first storm is a busy week for farmers and gophers, and could be a good one for Bobby Blue.

According to Greg the gopher man, gophers work in shifts. Four minutes of work is followed by four hours of rest. While sipping my morning coffee on our deck and watching a session of intense dirt-pushing, that seems pretty accurate. Those four minutes spent above ground are as satisfying for a gopher as leaving my desk to hang the laundry on the line is for me. We can both enjoy the clover that is reemerging after the first winter rain. It is green and nourishing for body and soul, just what is needed on an early-winter's morning.

Bobby Blue is a young blue heron entering his first season since hatching. He is also watching the ground moving. As with all teenagers, this is his most dangerous and critical time. Only thirty-three percent of his generation will survive to maturity. If he learns to hunt successfully through the upcoming winter, and has luck, he can look forward to fifteen years on the lagoon and its surrounds, and maybe even a long and happy marriage. But today, he must first find breakfast.

During the last few days of Indian summer, Mickey plowed under and freshly planted the front field with young brassicas. Now the gophers have moved back in, trying not to share their family's secrets of tender cabbage, broccoli, and kohlrabi. There is movement to the underground soil suburbs as the youngsters take over the homes of their elders on the ill-kept lawns and hill pastures of our farm. Territory is important for gophers and herons alike, and there are as many fights and uproars underground as there are noisy squabbles in the air. We cannot hear what goes on below, but Bobby Blue can. He is learning to read the signs of the changing underground city population.

At dawn, he spied fresh mounds of dirt in the old riding arena and flew down, landing softly on the grass. He felt the soil's vibrations and knew to follow where there was movement. By morning, Bobby had stepped closer to the activity he sensed was happening. Now he watched as the earth was pushed out in strong, staccato pulse-beats. His head was raised so that only his white throat reflects down, hiding his body from weak gopher eyes. The gopher kept pushing the dirt out, and with each shove, his head emerged further from the hole. This was a grand-old-daddy gopher reclaiming his den. The sunlight's glare temporarily blinded his shiny black eyes and though he wanted to adjust, to take in the bounty of green clover and check for danger, he knew he must be quick. Bobby needed to be quicker still. His dagger-tipped beak struck once, twice, and again, and he often missed. When the old gopher retreated, Bobby drew his head back too, but now there was blood on Bobby's bill. They each waited... but the gopher's work schedule is relentless and inflexible. Instinct drove him, and he pushed more dirt up and out and was vulnerable once more. It was as if he had forgotten the pain of the stab.

So it happened, again and again. The possessed gopher kept on pushing dirt out of his burrow and Bobby kept stabbing, trying to get a grip on the gopher and pull him up. This grandpapa gopher was heavy, fat, and strong and there was no way he was coming up and out easily. Bobby, by contrast, was young, still a lightweight, and not yet a skilled hunter. Finally, with one good strike, he grabbed the gopher on the back of his head and pulled. The gopher's strong front legs held onto the lip of the clover-bound grass and his weight almost tipped Bobby over. Bobby bent his hocks and spread his wings out for balance, trying not to fall forward completely. This dance, for it was a dance driven by the pulsing, instinctive rhythm of hunter and prey, continued long past the gopher's four-minute allotted timespan above ground. (By now I am well into my second cup of coffee, watching from the deck.) Slowly, the old gopher tired. He was bleeding from his head and would eventually die from his wounds even if he retreated. But for Bobby to eat his breakfast, the gopher must be brought from his hole. It was another five minutes, at least, before that was accomplished.

The gopher lay stunned on the ground. He turned, and snapping and flashing his big yellow teeth, trying to guard his life against Bobby but his death was assured. Bobby reached down, plucked the gopher up, and tossed him in the air to catch him with a better grip on his body. Carefully, Bobby then flew up and landed on a fencepost above the arena. Here he perched and paused, gopher in beak, while struggling to keep his balance and think about what to do next.

Again, size and weight confounded him. His youth and slight build were still a disadvantage with this huge gopher. (Choking on fish that are too big is also a known cause of death for herons.) A gopher's bones have to be crushed more completely before the body can be swallowed. This was the first grandpa Bobby had caught. Slowly, the weight of the gopher in his beak pulled his head lower and lower. His whole body dipped and swayed as he tried to stay upright and on his perch. Over time, if he lives, he will learn how to do this and stay balanced. But he does not yet have the strength or knowledge to lift his neck and head to toss and catch the gopher more deeply in his beak. He tried again, but became unbalanced, and the gopher fell into the grass arena. There was a pause while Bobby rested. The ancient patterns of hunt, kill, and consume have not yet been laid deeply enough. His instinctive rhythm had been disturbed. Hunger was there constantly, but now, so was fatigue. The gopher lay dead. Bobby flew down and stared at the motionless brown body. He was confused by its stillness. If it didn't move, he would no longer strike to kill. Slowly he walked away, lifting and placing each leg carefully, while looking for movement elsewhere in the lush grass.

Other birds had been watching. The ever-alert red-winged blackbirds were the first to dive. Next swooped the crows, ever on the hunt for free food. A vulture, perched on a telephone pole across the road, turned his head this way and that. Bobby was startled by the blackbird's attack on him, and, raising his wings and folding his neck, he took off from the grass arena and flew across the open field. The crows, now gathered into a murder, quickly overtook the blackbirds and pursued Bobby for the addictive fun of the chase. The hunter was now the hunted. He screeched his surprise and anger, which they returned with mocking, insulting cawing as they bombarded him across the pasture toward the school. The vulture waited until heron, blackbirds, and crows had flown across the two fields, heading toward the lagoon. Only then did he glide down from the telephone pole to stand and stare at the brown body lying still in the arena below.

Biking the Y.

The bike is ready and waiting for me each time I return to the farm. For a few mornings after my return, because of the time change from London to California, I am up at the very first light. Hanging in the closet is my forty-five-year-old jacket, now held together with duct tape. Somewhere I will find Bea's old St. Nicholas School beret and pull it down close over my head. St. Nicholas is the patron saint of the school that, thirty-six years apart, Beatrice and I both attended in Hampshire. St. Nic is the protector of children and sailors, and I like to think that biking around the edge of the lagoon counts as a sort of sailing. There may be mittens, or not. If I left them in the bicycle basket and the mice found them, they will have made a nest and I will need to knit new ones. Walter TY has made the bike ready; the tires are pumped tight, the few gears oiled, and the brakes checked. He knows the bike is my delight.

Bikes last a long time here, and this is only the fourth I have owned in the fifty years on the farm. It is from Mike Varley at Black Mountain Cycles in Point Reyes Station and was a birthday present from Walter in 2011. Mike's bike shop is small, tucked at the back of rough ground that doubles as a parking lot at the south end of town. It is crammed full of new bikes and parts of bikes and bike accessories. All bikers to West Marin, of which there are hundreds, if not thousands, passing though town on the weekends and more, know about Mike's Black Mountain Cycles shop. Mike is, naturally, a serious biker and has found the perfect niche here in West Marin. He is also (as importantly) a programmer at KWMR radio. He and our station manager, Amanda Eichstaedt, talk bikes—a lot.

This bike, my bike, is very low-key. Not quite a sit-up-and-beg bike, but it is very ordinary, has six gears, and could (in past years) get me up both sides of Phinney's Hill going in and out of town. I bike steadily, pedaling more slowly each year, but I keep pedaling. The three miles to the Y and back used to take me just twenty minutes; now it is twenty-seven minutes. But I don't mind. There is time to see the new life emerging while watching the old fallen eucalyptus tree sink deeper into the lagoon mud.

The mornings are laid out before me, unfolding into spring, summer, autumn, and winter. I draw courage from the life force in the seasons as they adjust to the climate changes we see, and take strength from the resistance and adaption of nature in this small corner of the world. I bike along the edge of the lagoon, on my way to the Y, where the unmarked road to Bolinas leaves Route One. The willows let loose on the little bird sanctuary north of Gospel Flat Farms are growing tall, persistently battering the eucalyptus trees for sun and taking root in the marsh edgings, creeping into the lagoon. On the other side of Route One is another unmarked road, up the ridge to Alpine Dam and over to Fairfax, but we don't talk about that road in quite the same familiar way.

For a brief while, the green bracken fonds are bright, light green, and tightly curled before slowly unfurling, ready to welcome an early spring to the roadside, then months pass until in the autumn, they crumble into coffee cream. In late spring and through the summer, the house wren cock, Troglodytes aedon, flits from one side of the road to the other as he sweet-talks and tempts a Jenny wren into his half–finished nest. He is a cruiser, with a sales pitch: "Here, try this one on the bank, or do you prefer the lagoon view?" He will build more than one nest, tempting whichever Jenny he can to mate with him. I like to think of him keeping his ladies separated by the road; one or two on the banks, another one or two on the lagoon. But it is hard work keeping so many ladies happy and he doesn't stay around to help with the families. The Jenny wrens have to do most of the heavy lifting: finishing the nest building, laying and sitting on the eggs, then raising the young. No wonder they flit so hurriedly back and forth across the road.

In summer, you can see the clear territorial line between the blue scrub jays and the Stellar's jays. The scrub jays stay south of Ed Letter's old house, towards Bolinas. The Stellar's jays stay north of Art Carpenter's Round House. Both are loud in defending their territory. The scrub jays claim the oak trees, the Stellar's jays the pines, and if there is a squabble, it can take place in the eucalyptus trees. As the temperature changes in these last years, the Stellar's jays have come further south and are found in town and on the mesa.

If the tide has been a winter-high king tide, there may be young sea otters in the tiny pond where the roadside ditch, taking the hillside runoff of winter-storm water, lingers, swirling for a pause before going under the road. This is where I stop for fresh watercress.

While I bike slower, the cars that pass me seem to go even faster than before. And still, every winter, someone misreads the camber of the road and gouges deep into the corner ditches by Bill Albright's old place, now John Borg's, on one side and Mickey Murch's Gospel Flat Farms stand on the other. Every winter. The traffic has picked up such speed and volume, and the parks have closed many of their gates to the wilderness, so no one rides their horses briskly on the verge out to Route One. The Horseshoe Hill Loop was a perfect stretch on those stormy days when horses were stalled yet needed a good trot out. Now, drivers don't even stop to ask for directions. There is no longer a need for the exchanges,

"Do you know the way to the town?"

"Yes." And I got ready to pedal on.

Maybe they would pause—and try again.

"Good morning... good afternoon... excuse me... Could you tell me the way to town, to the trailhead, the surf? Is there a gas station here, there?"

"Certainly," and I give them the information they ask for, and probably because I chatter, a little bit more...

The GPS has taken away from us another reason, or excuse, to interact with each other.

Drivers have apps and maps and Yelp telling them where the beaches are and how the surf is today, and so they put their pedal to the metal as maybe I did, on stolen Saturday dawn mornings for a year, a young mother with four children driving the motorway from London to the country, with the same hunger for two hours riding and the smell of sweat in the horse barn as these surfers search out the sea. They whizz through those (our) still country lanes with little thought or regard for who else shares the road or wants to cross it from time to time.

The creatures have learned to be cautious. The whine of a fast car is a signal to scurry back into the underbrush and brambles because something not quite in control is out and about. The morning air is still and chilled when I ride my bike early enough to see the disappearing dawn feeders. Coming around the bottom side of the Y, where the unmarked roads into and out of town meet Route One, a young rabbit hops into the uncut roadside brush, leaving just his white bunny bottom sticking out. He sits very still until I ride past and then, I hope, he keeps going into the Y triangle. There is a crackle of twigs and flicking of another white bobtail as a young doe also makes her way back into that patch. This is all I see disappearing into the triangle of scrub that fills the Y turn. It remains a refuge for creatures great and small. I love to see them go in and rest, sheltered from the wind if it is a cold, foggy day or from the sun if it is hot. But not everyone learns the lesson—the youngsters, the brave, and the unaware may not heed a car and then disaster strikes.

Roadkill

A truck is parked beside the lagoon, a woman running away from it, back along the road to the creek. It is Hilary Smith from Dogtown.

"Ali said she hit something last night." We look together and quickly Hilary finds the body. It is a big old dog fox, with a huge brush on him and plenty of red in his coat. His eyes bulge from a head wound. His mouth is twisted and agape from a smashed jaw. His belly is full of apples or disease or bloated from starvation. Maybe he was older and getting a little deaf, as we do. I pick him up. He must weigh fifteen-plus pounds, and I carry him a little away into the underbrush.

By midmorning the vultures are well into him. They take turns, seemingly patient in their queueing, high up in the trees, watching those who go first take as long they need pecking at the carcass. It the biggest, pushiest birds who stuff themselves until they can barely fly back to the lowest branches of willow trees curbing the road. Counting vultures is like looking at big black flower heads. First I see eight, then twelve, then twenty. The fox's belly is ripped open. The, soft blood-filled organs are devoured first. The head lies back, the eyes are gone, and a channel is made to the brain. In only three days, the shell alone remains; skin, some skull and bones, and the beautiful brush are all that is left. The vultures now fly higher, ever watching for more signs and smelling the air for death.

Lagoon Kill

The morning mist is still low on the ground as I bike over the little bridge and around the corner to the lagoon, past where the early-morning birders park their cars. The tide is low right now and there is a moving mass in the mud. I stop the bike and rest my feet on the road to watch. A coyote is nipping and ripping at a carcass. I'm too far away to see exactly, but it looks like a seal; not a pup, but not full-grown either, an adolescent coming to an early end. How so? Nipped by a shark, a teenage pregnancy, or a man-induced disease? As I lower the kickstand of my bike down onto the pavement, the coyote lifts his head. He hears, then sees me, and smartly trots away along the mud. I have missed my photo-op moment. Back on the bike, I pedal slowly along, watching for and seeing him under the willows, on the marsh grass, and sense that all that time he is watching me. On my return, I look for him again but there is only a lone vulture sitting on a low branch, his solid-black back turned to me as he faces the carcass, preparing for his place at the table.

A week later, the carcass is but a spine with ribs. The single vulture has long been joined by others of the corvid family: crows, rooks, and ravens. They sit on the mud-covered spine and pluck the salted flesh, each in their turn.

A Glancing Blow

This day, the day I collect these memories, biking slowly, being passed by cars quickly, the sun is shining on the road ahead and lying in front of me is a glistening light bay-brown blob. As I come alongside I am surprised and sad to see it is a weasel. Weasels are shy creatures, cautious and quick, and it is rare to glimpse them. But when we do, they are busy, scurrying back into the hedgerows after a field hunt. They are tidy too, and it is easy to miss the signs of their predation. Though tiny, the least weasel can catch and bring home a good-sized gopher and so we are grateful to know they are around. But this little blob is lying still in the middle of the road. He is so beautiful. I stop to pay homage to his death, to move him out of the way of the cars that are racing and circling out from behind me. Putting the bike to the side of the road, I bend over him and find that his little tummy is still going up and down, up and down. Plucking comfrey (Symphytum) leaves from the roadside verge, I put them in the bicycle basket and then lift him up off the road and place him on the leaves. He is still, stunned yet breathing. Mounting my bike again as the cars speed past, I pedal the last few yards home. Now, parked in the driveway, I can look down in the basket and at my patient. It takes only a few moments for him to realize the movement has stopped. There is blood on his head, but his eyes are bright when he opens them and blinks a few times. In a little while he stretches up, his front paws resting on the bike handles for a minute or two, and he looks around, taking in the situation. A decision is made and he looks at me as if to say, "Thanks for that. It was only a glancing blow." And he pushes off, jumping down from the bike and scampering away to the honeysuckle vine across the field. He is ready to cross the road one more time.

Unbearable Made Bearable

The lace curtains will not survive even one more gentle handwashing. The California sun has bleached away the color and now the threads are parting. They have hung in the upstairs bathroom and big bedroom, away from the direct harshness of the sun, but they are dying and it is time to take them down. Standing on a chair unaided, while I still can, I take them off the rods and let the sunlight rudely intrude on our privacy. The curtains are overflowing yet light in my arms. Moving quickly, not waiting for second thoughts, I hurry downstairs and outside, through the barn and to the field beyond. There I lay them like cobweb shrouds onto the compost piles. They cover the detritus of the farm that will grow new life out of death. They are twenty-eight years old.

★ ★ ★

A plane from London to Paris, then a train on to Geneva took me to where *The Unbearable Lightness of Being* was filming. Like an invading Roman army, the film crew had set up camp in the city. The hotels were their tents, the cars their chariots, propelling cast and crew members to the battlefield of the set. It may have been on *White Dawn* or this film that Phil Kaufman uttered the memorable phrase, "Fun is the past tense of shit." I don't really remember. Each film creates a moving caravan of traveling people who join together for this endeavor, coming to know each other as deeply as any family. Married and united for this budgeted time, for better or worse. There are requited, or not, love affairs that must bloom in order for the filming to take place. The dog was a particular favorite for this film. The crews operated in their own battalions and were often billeted together in the same hotel.

There are soft memories of wandering the streets of Geneva, walking with other members of the cast or crew but mostly alone. The autumnal mornings were sunny, the air clear and fresh. And when finding myself in front of a bright store window full of Swiss lace, I clicked the door latch down and entered. The owner's smile held steady as I smiled and apologized that I spoke only English. Her sigh at my incomplete education was suppressed, maybe knowing there was a film crew in the city and that there were bound to be surplus wives, lost and aimless. The curtains that were hung in the window had caught me with their colors, gentle and diffuse pastels, like the Swiss themselves. A fresh package was produced from a shelf and put on the counter. Swiss francs changed hands. I packed it into my suitcase and brought the new curtains back to the farm.

The story of *The Unbearable Lightness of Being* draws to a close as Sabina, living and painting in her old farmhouse, is visited by an older couple who live close by and have befriended her. She is a lone artist and refugee, and they know a refugee's story. The older couple and Sabina bring each other comfort and peace in this twilight relationship. It is here that the postman brings Sabina news of the death of her lover, Tomas, and his wife, Tereza, also her lover.

Here was the farm for three days. The house is stripped down, back to how it looked when we first arrived in 1972. Walking into the living room, I stood in shock, wondering if I had managed to make any progress in homemaking at all. The production crew had taken over and I retreated to the barn or the hills. But as the last day winds down, it is definitely time for tea. Lena Olin, who gave birth four months before filming began, is upstairs with her baby and the nanny. Marrian Walters and Niven Busch, who play the older neighbors who have come to visit Sabina, are sitting uncomfortably at the kitchen table. Such is an actor's lot. The house is not warm, and even in summertime a chill enters the kitchen. It is time to put the kettle on and make some tea. The first of my mother's Blue Willow china offloads are brought out. (There were to be many more offloads from my mother as she continued to buy Booth Blue Willow to replace what she had already given me.) She was right; the Blue Willow did add something to the style of the farm, but there were to be a great many dinner plates, finally a full set, before she stopped. Huddling close to the stove, Niven is perched on a leather-and-wood three-legged stool. He and the stool looked none too steady. With a discreet inquiry, I ask if he would like something a little stronger than tea. It is clear that he does. The pot of tea is made and poured. The sherry bottle comes to the table, along with lemon and sugar. Some cups are filled with tea and the others with sherry. On the table it is hard to tell them apart, and at this point nobody really cares. Niven takes a sip of sherry. "What is the name of this film, anyway?"

"*The Unbearable Lightness of Being*," I reply.

There is a short pause before he takes another longer sip.

"The only thing worse than that would be *Closed for Repairs*." The sherry bottle empties at the same rate as the teapot before the last take is safely in the camera, the light dims, and the call goes out from the assistant director, "That's a wrap."

Already the crew have been quietly dismantling their equipment. Putting electric cables in cases, makeup brushes in boxes. The cars are ready to take the cast back to the city. The producers leave too, next the director as the house is put back into order. And, suddenly, they are all gone. The house is empty, cold, and we, the house and I, feel a little bewildered. What was all that activity? Where did they all go, and will they ever return? No. Not to the house, but the next day, horses and pony-clubbers gathered at Stinson Beach where the bright autumn California sun and Pacific Ocean played a final melody in harmony with the paler light of Czechoslovakia.

Reclaiming the house from the filming, along with the unnecessary cleaning that followed, called for something, a treat with which to gift the house. The lace curtains were unpacked, light curtain rods were put in place, and the soft Swiss lace hung gently, caressing the tall windows of the south walls. Their colored hems were a reminder of another way of being, a light way, a gentle but strong way that held us in sleep, allowing the moon and starlight to shine softly on our bed.

A few weeks later, a handy check arrived, and I could now afford the gravel and sand much needed for a dressage riding arena.

After the final double truck-and-trailer load is delivered and spread, Clyde and his son come into the kitchen for a pot of coffee. Interestingly, they sit at either end of the kitchen table, far away from each other. Clyde looks over at me and through his son. His son looks dazed, hunched in a perpetual crouch. He doesn't speak at all. Business is taken care of and then, leaving the double-load trailer by the roadside, they take the big rig up to Sally at Vanishing Point Ranch to see how much sand / gravel she might need for her arena. They chat, as one does. And then he passes his verdict on us all.

"Now, your friend, Aggie. She been rode hard and put away wet."

Sally kept a straight face until we shared and compared our visits of Clyde and his mute son. The river-gravel fell easily into the two ranches' arenas, where children and adults rode and grew together.

★ ★ ★

The Swiss lace curtains are gone now. Faded into soil and regrowth. But there is nothing comparable in style or price to be found in the city. Even the newer, upmarket home-beautiful stores that are now the bibles for mall and catalogue shoppers hold nothing that lifts my spirits. They are useful, and the best that America has to offer, and so, resignedly, I bring two pairs home. The curtain rods are still strong and I can put up the new curtains on those south-facing windows. They are somber, plain, utilitarian, ready to do their job, but add nothing to the sweet beauty of the strong Indian silk over-blinds. They hang like maiden aunts who live in Hove, standing next to their more exotic cousins from Brighton. They carry no mystery of a different seduction. Even the moonlight is shy to show herself. I pause and look around the room once more. Then it is time to close the door and make my way downstairs.

Chapter 13

Who Carries the Seed?

In the late 1970s, searching out locations in Tennessee for his film *Harvest*, filmmaker-turned-farmer Carroll Ballard pulled up at a general feed store in Knoxville and went inside. Soon he was sipping coffee with four, five, or six farmers sitting around the barrels of seeds. While talking slowly, some smoking steadily, each farmer sat with one hand in the seed barrel, continually running his fingers through the seeds. It seemed sensual, said Carroll, as if they were caressing a maiden's hair, gently testing her; was she ready for their complete embrace? By touch and by smell, they could tell when the seed was good, ripe, and ready for planting. Only then would they buy. When the time came, not many words would be exchanged, maybe, "I reckon I'll take two sacks of clover and alfalfa, one of sunflower." Whatever sacks were chosen would then be pulled out from the circle and sealed. Dollars or credit changed hands before the sacks were loaded into a wagon, cart, or truck.

In due course, it would be time to plant the seeds of grasses, legumes, flowers, and potatoes. If the goddesses Demeter, Ceres, Saranya, or Renenutet felt honored, then growth and harvest would follow.

Also to be considered were the soil, the weather, and the time of year. To know those things takes a seed of a different kind, the seed that germinates within the soul. What part of the DNA will produce the farmer? For the seed must be present for passion to grow into a life's calling that cannot be denied, be it artist, scientist, fisherman, or farmer. Nurturing is important, but there is no guarantee that our seeds will flourish. This is true for filmmakers and farmers both. Carroll Ballard has made films that will remain classics in film history. Among them the aforementioned *Harvest*, my favorite, *Rodeo, Fly Away Home, Never Cry Wolf,* and *The Black Stallion* being the most notable one of them. But he also became a vintner, growing with his wife, Christina, a particularly fine grape that is much sought-after by other vintners. There were two separate paths for his daughter to choose. It was to be film.

Within families, there is a long-distance call for the children we have begotten to continue what we have built. A longing for our work to continue after our death; for it, our lives, not to have been lived in vain. Few of us are truly content with the wishes of Galsworthy's Young Jolyon in the first part of *The Forsyte Saga*—to be remembered with love. We crave more, not to be discarded, dust to dust, ashes to ashes. "Hold me a little longer" is our ongoing, outgoing call. Submerged or overt, it is there. What will happen to our knowledge, the talent, the physical structures we have built? We remember when our parents were born and died, but rarely can we date our grandparents in the same way. This question must linger somewhere within the Martinelli, Dierks, Murch, Weber, Murch, and Tacherra families. All are deep-seated farmers, some of four generations, some just one. It is an open question, only pressed into needing an answer by the value of farming, desire, the land itself, and our communities. Who carries this in their blood and heart is a question that all old family farmers ask among themselves. Who of their children, and their children's children, will carry on farming their land? Who has the gene and the passion that can be nurtured to keep the family farms and agriculture going forward, combining old and new ways of farming? It is maybe the biggest question and concern for farmers who love their land, work, and families in equal measure, and for all those who create physical, tangible dynasties.

Epilogue

April 2021

That spring in England was cold, with more hard ground frost than has been recorded in the last sixty years. And it was dry. There were few April showers to bring forth those expected, rhyming May flowers. The yellow daffodils bloomed but did not linger on the grassy lawns of Regent's Park or the wilder hillsides of Hampstead Heath. They faded quickly and gave way to seemingly reluctant, sharp red tulips nestled in forget-me-nots and skirted with violets and primroses. But the bluebells carpeted the woodlands and lingered a while, grateful that the sun is weak and filtered through the trees.

It is different on the farm from where Sirima sends almost-daily pictures. The barn wisteria is blooming and swaying in the spring breeze. The birds have returned, are pairing and nesting. Chickens and chicks are safe in the apple orchard. New bee swarms have been caught to replace the ones that left after last summer's fires that swept through Point Reyes, West Marin, and beyond. Sheep are grazing in the pastures as there used to be in Mrs. Peters's time. Twin lambs are bringing laughter to a restful happy hour. The roses are blooming earlier and earlier as the weather patterns change throughout the world. The gophers are busy below ground while the sap begins to rise in the fruit trees, swelling the buds that will burst into blossom. A new season has begun.

PHOTOGRAPHS

Chard in winter: The chard is bowed down to the ground with the weight of shinny crystals, the broccoli looks like it was hit in a fight and the fennel is weeping icy tears of cold. When I return from my bike ride the sun has moved over the field and the chard has shaken off its pessimism and is rising, shining to meet the new day.

Persimmon bowl.

Water Cress beginning.

Houseboat early days.

Houseboat thoughts.

From this to that - Houseboat finished. Photo by Bernard André used with permission.

Raising the Greenhouse at Blackberry Farm with family and friends. Carroll Ballard, Aggie, Pam Goodman, Janet, Matthew and Sonya Robbins. Alicia Law, Barbara and Hal Barwood, Mary Jo Deschanel Marcia and George Lucas, Tom Scott, Jon and Toby Barwood, Walter Slater Murch, Ted Young, Beatrice Murch and Johan. Photo by Caleb Deschanel.

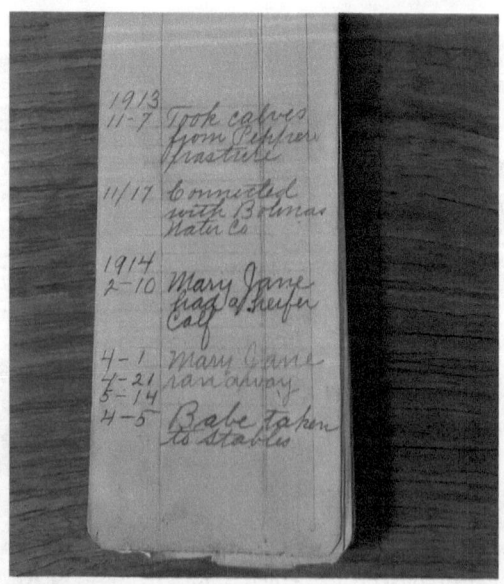

Mr. Smith's Notebook. The same size as the modern mobile phone.

Ed Letters old house.

Pancakes Galore Prices 1974.

Walter at the Well.

WSM makes an Announcement. George looks on.

Apple Bobbing becomes Bobbing for Smitches.

Viv turns Barrel Racing to Speed Splicing.

Worst Hand Anyway.

Wisteria blossoms hang low and their scent is heavy around the barn. Soon the bright green leaves will follow, rising to shroud the mauve blooms as death overtakes them.

Lovely working worms and cooking compost.

Bea in her daffodil yellow dress among the early spring daffodils 1976.

A smiling Phil peaking through us.

Pacific Slope goes to Cannes with MAM and executive producer Trish Hoffman.

The Borage, poppies and calendula call the bees now that spring is here.

Rhubarb ready for sale.

Cosimo Ballard spoons straight from the bowl. Never any left overs.

Babe fitted with her microphones by WSM. Carrie in the saddle ready to record.

Babe and Connie roping.

Babe and her girls: Babe's New Penny, Carrie, Connie, Beth, Bea and Aggie.

Suddenly the Naked Ladies are in bloom.

Grosso lavender ready for sale.

Three Radio Gals at Blackberry Farm, January 2005. Susan Stone KPFA Pacifica, Nicole Sawaya KPFA Pacifica and KALW, Muriel/Aggie Murch KPFA Pacifica and KWMR.org.

Someone brings me his blackberry harvest for all sorts of treats.

Black Berry Surprise

Black Berry Farm, Bolinas, Ca.

1 quart berries   serves 6-8
¼ lb. melted butter
bread strips
1 c. sugar
2 Tbsp. flour
lemon juice

❖ Grease bottom of dish. Cover with bread strips
  soaked in butter. Add berry mixture & cover
  with thatched bread strips.
❖ Bake at 350° 25-30 minutes.
❖ Serve warm over vanilla ice cream. Enjoy.

Blackberry Surprise recipe.

Blackberry Surprise ready for ice cream.

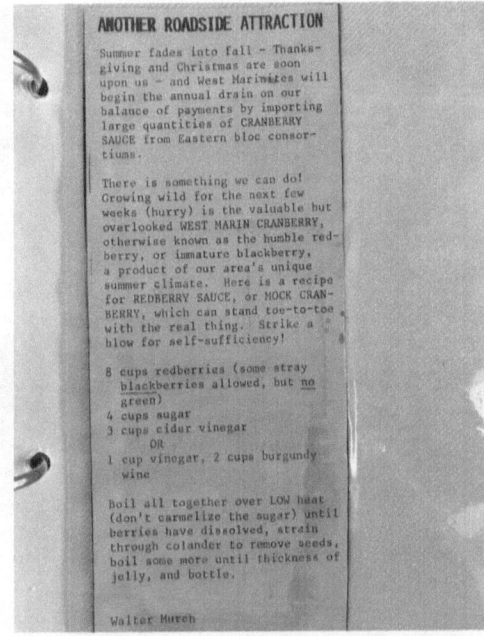

ANOTHER ROADSIDE ATTRACTION

Summer fades into fall – Thanksgiving and Christmas are soon
upon us – and West Marinites will
begin the annual drain on our
balance of payments by importing
large quantities of CRANBERRY
SAUCE from Eastern bloc consor-
tiums.

There is something we can do!
Growing wild for the next few
weeks (hurry) is the valuable but
overlooked WEST MARIN CRANBERRY,
otherwise known as the humble redberry, or immature blackberry,
a product of our area's unique
summer climate. Here is a recipe
for REDBERRY SAUCE, or MOCK CRAN-
BERRY, which can stand toe-to-toe
with the real thing. Strike a
blow for self-sufficiency!

8 cups redberries (some stray
   blackberries allowed, but no
   green)
4 cups sugar
3 cups cider vinegar
      OR
1 cup vinegar, 2 cups burgundy
   wine

Boil all together over LOW heat
(don't carmelize the sugar) until
berries have dissolved, strain
through colander to remove seeds,
boil some more until thickness of
jelly, and bottle.

Walter Murch

Another Roadside Attraction written by WSM and published in the Coastal
Poast.

Brian's Rose still undetermined.

Aggie and three chickens in the orchard.

Wisteria the chicken.

Little Richard and his wives.

A springtime Farm Harvest of eggs and Greengage plums.

Mickey springs a leak.

A helping hand.

Blueberry Cake.

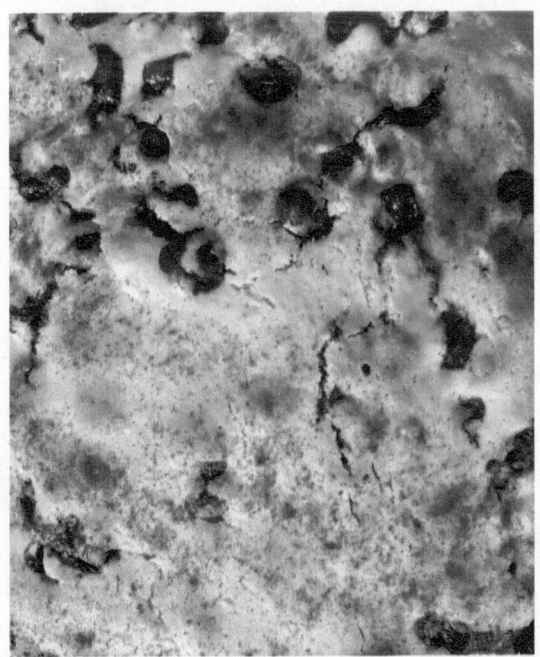

Blueberry cake close up reminds Walter of the surface of Io, one of Jupiter's moons. Well it would, wouldn't it?

Tiktok.

Ripening Hauer Pippins bow down the young tree.

Apple Harvest for pressing with Paul Brennan, John Perry and Walter TY prepping for the press 2006.

Aggie pouring juice with friends.

Aggie and Warren Webber pouring juice at the 2014 Apple Pressing – best year yet.

Beets for sale at the Gospel Flat farm stand.

Supper for one a simple Borscht soup.

Peter's gift. Mitzi admires Peter's strawberries.

Don's Alaskan turnips.

Don's crab pots waiting by the channel.

Crab catch of the day.

November frost.

Cartoon posted on the apple/bee shed wall. Noel Ford with permission from the Ford family.

Cider bottled and capped ready for that year's labels.

Young Bobby Blue. Photographed by Barbara Whitt used with her permission.

Biking the Y.

It was only a glancing blow.

Morning sky over the farm.

August 6, 1965.

Recipe Index

BIBLIOGRAPHY AND
REFERENCES

Aikenhead, Steve. *Group memories: School days in Bolinas and Stinson Beach*. Perfect Paperback, 1993.

Attenborough, Sir David. *The Private Life of Plants*. BBC Publishing, 1994.

'BB' *The Countryman's Bedside Book*. Eyrs & Spotiswoods, 1942.

'BB' *The Wayfaring Tree*. Hollis and Carter LTD, 1946.

Berger, John. *Pig Earth*. Pantheon Modern Writers, 1979.

Berger, John. *Once in Europa*. Pantheon Modern Writers, 1983.

Bernstein, Arlene. *Growing Season: Life Lessons from the Garden*. Council Oak Books, 2004.

Berry, Wendell. *The Unsettling of America: Culture and Agriculture*. Sierra Club Books, 1977.

Berry, Wendell. *The Art of Loading Brush*. Counterpoint LLC, 2018.

Brogdale Fruit Catalogue. Out of print and replaced by https://brogdalecollections.org/.

Business Wire. *Fast Company*. Lists Niman Ranch among the World's Most Innovative Companies, March 2023.

Card, F.W. *Bush Fruits*. from the Rural Science Series. The Macmillan Company, 1925. https://ediblemarinand-winecountry.ediblecommunities.com/food-thought/farmsteads-california-coast

Carson, Rachael. *Silent Spring*. Houghton Mifflin Company, 1962.

Churchman, Josh. *The Whale That Lit the World*. lulu.com, 2018.

Coppola, Eleanor. *Notes On a Life*. Nan A Tales, 2008.

Fiennes, Jake. *Land Healer*. Witness Books of Ebury, 2022.

Galsworthy, John. *The Forsyte Saga*. William Heinemann Ltd, 1922.

Gladwell, Malcolm. *The Crooked Ladder*. The New Yorker. August 11 & 18, 2014.

Gourmet Cookbook. Volume 2 Gourmet, Inc. 1957.

Grant, David. *The Seven-Year Hitch: A Family Odyssey*. Simon and Schuster, 1999.

Greenmantle Nursery http://www.greenmantlenursery.com/

Hahn, Nicolette. *Righteous Porkchop*. Harper Collins, 2009.

Hahn, Nicolette. *Defending Beef*. Chelsea Green, 2014.

Henry, Diana. *A Change of Appetite Where Healthy Meets Delicious*. Mitchell Beazley 2014.

Hirsch, Paul. Essay on the Droid Olympics. https://cinemontage. org/the-droid-olympics/

Hooper, Ted. *Guide to Bees and Honey*. Blandford Press Ltd., 1976.

Hubbell, Sue. *A Book of Bees; And How to Keep Them*. Houghton Mifflin Company, 1988.

Kimmey, Samantha. *"First Bolinas Farm MALTed"* Point *Reyes Light*: November 26th, 2014.

Knickerbocker, Peggy. *Simple Soirées*. Stewart, Tabon and Chang, 2005.

Langford, Sarah. *Rooted Stories of Life, Land and a Farming Revolution*. Viking Penguin Random House, 2022.

Langford, Sarah. *Agriculture reinvention has come to far to be threatened*. The Financial Times Weekend, October 8, 2022.

Leopold, Aldo. *A Sand Country Almanac* and *Sketches Here and There*. Penguin Classics, 2020.

Lewis-Stempel, John. *Meadowland: The Private Life of an English Field*. Black Swan, 2015.

Lewis-Stempel, John. *Still Water: The Deep Life of the Pond*. Black Swan, 2020.

Lewis-Stempil, John. *The Wild Life of the Fox.* Penguin Random House, 2020.

Lively, Penelope. *Life In the Garden.* Fig Tree 2017. https://www.marinij.com/2017/08/08/usf-buys-star-route-farms-in-bolinas-to-sustain-organic-farm-education/

Livingston, Douglas. *Ranching On the Point Reyes Peninsula: A History of the Dairy and Beef Ranches Within Point Reyes National Seashore, 1834-1992.* Point Reyes National Seashore, National Park Service. 1994.

Los Angeles Times *3 Acres of History: Center Seeks to Preserve Rare Varieties of Apples* July 26, 198712 am Associated Press.

Munroe-Fraser, J.P. *History of Marin County, California.* Alley, Bowen & Co. 1880, (illustrated). Republished Charmaine Burdell Veronda, 1972.

Ondaatje, Michael. *The Conversations Walter Murch and the Art of Film Making.* Knopf, 2003.

Orenstein, Peggy. *Unraveling: What I Learned About Life While Shearing Sheep, Dyeing Wool, and Making the World's Ugliest Sweater.* HarperCollins, 2023.

Pollan, Michael. *The Botany of Desire: A Plant's-Eye View of the World.* Random House, 2001.

Reader's Digest. *Encyclopedia of Garden Plants and Flowers.* 1987.

Rebanks, James. *English Pastoral An Inheritance.* Allen Lane, 2020. Penguin, 2021.

Rodale, J.I., Editor in Chief. *How to Grow Vegetables and Fruits by the Organic Method.* Rodale Books Inc., 1970.

Schell, Orville. *The Town that Fought to Save Itself.* Pantheon Books, 1976.

Seymour, John. *The Guide to Self Sufficiency.* Dorling Kindersley Ltd., 1975.

Singer, Fanny. *Always Home: A Daughter's Recipes and Stories.* Knopf, 2020.

Smit, Tim. *The Lost Gardens of Heligan.* Orionbooks.co.uk. 2010.

Steavenson, Wendell. *Dispatch from Lviv.* Financial Times Weekend, April 16/17 2022.

Stuart-Smith, Sue. *The Well Gardened Mind.* William Collins, 2020.

The Land an occasional magazine about land rights *Manifesto* and *A Short History of Enclosure in Britain.* Summer, 2009.

Euphon-Todd, Barbara. *Worzel Gummidge.* Puffin Books, 1936.

Waters, Alice. *Chez Panisse Menu Cookbook.* Random House, 1982.

Waters, Alice. *Coming To My Senses.* Clarkson Potter, 2017.

Credit: Billy Bob Thornton
Styling: Carrie Angland

ABOUT THE AUTHOR

MURIEL AGGIE MURCH is the author of *Journey in the Middle of the Road: One Woman's Path through a Midlife Education* and *The Bell Lap Stories for Compassionate Nursing Care*.

A founding member of KWMR.org, she continues to biweekly produce *Letter From A. Broad*. She lives with her husband in Northern California and London.

ACKNOWLEDGMENTS

"**D**arling, You remember Steve Wax?" Walter pushed through the crowd of Bay Area film folk gathered in the Zoetrope Café for the party to celebrate American Zoetrope's 50th birthday in 2019. Beside him was a very neat and dapper gentleman. Remember Steve? Yes. Recognize him? No way. Last seen, Steve was a wild young man with strong communist beliefs, a camera in hand, and no time for "wives of". But here he was, at his request, standing in front of me with something to say. After the "Hello, so good to see you, how are you?" I paused, not having a clue where this was going. Walter had disappeared back into the crowd, but I need not have worried; Steve had something on his mind. He had read some of my essays published in *The West Marin Review* and said how much he liked them. "They are beautiful." In that crowded café party, my nervousness led me to blurt out: "There are more." A few weeks later, we began weekly conversations on Zoom that have continued to this day. And each week we talked, he told me, "You have to write that." And to my amazement, I did. Memories and stories twisting and turning like an underground bubbling spring poured out onto the pages. Without Steve's consistent coaxing and encouragement, this book would not be in your hands, and to him, I owe the deepest gratitude.

I am also beyond a spade-depth grateful to everyone who read all, or bits of, this manuscript in its various chrysalis forms as it turned from caterpillar-like journal into memoir. It is because of your support and suggestions that it is emerging as the butterfly it is.

Wayne Alexander, Carrie Angland, Linda Delibero, Walter Donahue, Anne-Marie Feenberg-Dibon, Lyons Filmer, John Gouldthorpe, Carol and Dexter Hake, Peggy Knickerbocker, Beatrice Louise Murch, Don Murch, Walter Murch, Walter

Slater Murch, Davia Nelson, Doris Ober, Kate Rae, Gail Reitano, Sirima Sataman, Orville Schell, Susan Stone, Laurie Mahan Sawyer, Connie A. Thornton, and, obviously, the afore-mentioned Steve Wax.

Then there are those of you who helped with setting me to rights with your memories that proved sharper than my research. "Actually, Aggie, the van was blue." "The date was..." and many more from all your kind responses, each and every one with encouragement: Arden Bucklin, Michael Bernsohn, Jeff Creque, park ranger Loretta Farley, shared her knowledge of the coastal tribes of West Marin, Greg and Randy (Coon) Fontan, Keith Hansen, Tim and Alex Horvath, Elia Haworth, Phil and Peter Kaufman, Peter Martinelli, Mel and Tinker Pervier, Mary Siedman, Bill, Jim and Susan Tacherra, and Jean Wright. Keith Hansen shared his knowledge of the behavior and characteristics of our resident and visiting birds. Kate Ray fed me copious writings from Aldo Leopold and John Lewis-Stempel, which led, naturally, to the work of BB. Those of you who love old farm literature will be happy to follow me down this rabbet warren of literature. Beatrice Murch (firmly) reminded her mother that if you don't ask, you have an automatic No. Bea joined Ali Musa in keeping my computers (there were two) and I calmly and con-stantly backed up. Thank you both.

Sean Thackrey (1943-2022) brought me medieval texts, encouraged, applauded, and then drank my cider and pronounced it, "Good. Yes, that's very good, Aggie." How I wish he was here today to enjoy the fruits of this harvest. Sean was a strong warp in the fabric of our town's weaving. Greg Watson, master sailor that he is, taught me a maritime knot or two while with his unerring sense of the sea's currents, winds, and whirlpools helped guide our farm into a safer harbor for the next chapter of its existence. May Blackberry Farm stay upright and weather the storms that are always on the world's horizon.

More than one reader will find an error or even two that will have slipped in between words and memory. I apologize, but there they must sit for the moment.

Wayne Alexander handed me to agent Murray Weiss, who graciously took *Harvesting* under his wing. Supportive from the get-go, kindly, and responsive, Murray got to work, I suspect hiding the "Thanks but no thanks" rejections out of my sight, yet sharing the more kindly ones before *Harvesting History* found a home with Sibylline Press and All Things Book. Publisher Vicki DeArmon is a powerhouse in her support of women writers of a certain age and the readers of all ages who are helping this publisher grow on the national stage. I sometimes think Vicki must have inherited the energy and excitement that Carmen Callie felt when she published Virago's first book in 1973. Thank you for being such a team.

And the editors. Lyons Filmer, how wonderful that you have been a part of this journey. Thank you for your early encouragement and grammatical eagle eye, balanced by your ever-aware ear for my voice. Walter Donahue read and reread the manuscript, seeing it had a beginning, middle, and an end but that they were not necessarily in that order. He gently yet firmly tacked my vessel of words into the wind, on course, until he was able to say, *"Yes, it is all here. This is how a book of the land should be."* A phone message left on a barely used phone and finally returned led to a conversation with Clive Stränger. Clive had once been kind enough to join a lone lady having her afternoon tea at the Beverly Wilshire Hotel. Lightly, we kept in touch and on this phone call he asked the question, *"What are you doing now?"* His follow-up emails introduced me to Sarah Hochman, who also embraced *Harvesting* and has stayed with me through to this end. With her firm but gentle guidance (how I love firm but gentle guidance), words no longer needed were pruned away and those remaining flowed more smoothly along the page. Now, in this almost final edit, it is Jennifer Safrey who combed through my words bringing *Harvesting* to completion. To you all, I am grateful beyond measure.

Our family, Walter TY, Beatrice, Carrie, and Connie, all with families of their own, have kept an eye and ear out for Mum and her *Harvesting* as they went on their way with their lives. Throughout, Walter the grayer, the elder, the editor, stayed by my side. While in the Covid years in London, we were both writing our stories, leaving pages for each other on the table, a chair, or the bed. Constantly, he gave me courage to "try this" while he scattered (more) commas, along with encouragement, as liberally as rose petals on a lover's bed. Thank you.

Family, friends, farms, and films woven into the pages:

<u>Family</u>

Walter Murch
Walter TY Murch
Beatrice Murch
Carrie Angland
Connie Angland
Granny Slater
Sirima Sataman
Tom Scott

<u>Friends and Folks</u>

Mike Aiken
Steve Aikenhead
Rosie Barry
Michael Bernsohn

Patricia Briceño
Joss Churchman
Jeff Creque
Don Deane
Dave Duffin
Perry Fly
Coon Fontain
David Grant and Family
Sasha Gold
Carol and Dexter Hake
Keith Hansen
Horvath Brothers
Dr. Arnold Kegal
Rick Klaes
Peggy Knickerbocker
Robbie Knowles
Harriet Kossman
Ed Letter
Gurukar and Susan Martinelli
Ben and Meitty Meyer
Don, Sarah and Mickey Murch
Chuck Oakander
Sally Peacock
Cretta Pullen
Gail Reitano
Sherman Smith
Jessie Swartz
Jesse Tacherra
Lydia Tacherra
Orville Schell
Mike Varley
Mike Whitt

Farms and their farmers

Blackberry Farm — Aggie Murch
Fresh Run Farm — Peter Martinelli
Gospel Flat Farms — Don and Mickey Murch
Niman Ranch — Bill and Nicolette Hahn Niman
Paradise Valley — Dennis and Sandra Dieks
Star Route Farm — Warren Weber Annabelle Lenderink
Tacherra Ranch — Jesse, Lydia and Jim

Radio world

Erik Bauersfeld
Kay Clements
Amanda Eichstaedt
Lyons Filmer
Susan Stone
Nicole Sawaya

Film makers

Carroll Ballard
Brad Bird
Ellie Coppola
Francis Coppola
Robert Dalva
Sara Fgaier
Vibeke Gad
Vivian Hillgrove
Pete Horner
Phil Kaufman

Mark Levinson
George Lucas
Anthony Mingella
Walter Murch
Michael Ondaatje
Hans-Erik Philip
Matthew Robbins
Alan Splet and Anne Kroeber
Randy Thom
Fred Zinneman

And some of their films:

American Graffiti
Apocalypse Now
The Black Stallion
The Conversation
Dragon Slayer
The English Patient
Ghost
The Godfather
Harvest
Hemmingway and Gellhorn
Julia
Particle Fever
The Rain People
Return to Oz
TomorrowLand
Touch of Evil
The Unbearable Lightness of Being

The following essays were previously published in various forms:

- "Lydia Tacherra Grand Mother," first published in *The Coastal Post*, 1995. And later excerpted for The Bolinas Museum farming exhibit, 2016.

- "Bolinas Rod and Boat Club Pancake Breakfasts," first read for Eat Your Heart Out, KWMR fundraiser April 2014.

- The Willow Woods and Friday, February 7, 2014 first published in the *West Marin Review*, Volume 9 2019. Friends and Neighbors, Black Mountain Circle, and Point Reyes Books.

The Map

The Map is by Laurie Mahan Sawyer of Point Reyes. Laurie immediately understood the need of a map. As she drew, the intent of it came clear and memories overflowed into the streams.

Permissions

Quote from Wendell Berry with kind permission from Wendell Berry.

Stancombe Cider cartoon by Noel Ford with kind permission from the Ford Family.

Photograph credits with permissions

Taghi Amirani

Postcard photo of the Houseboat community, Bernard Andre

Cosimo Ballard from Colin Ballard

Blackberry Farm Murch family archive

Vivian Hillgrove (we don't know which are Vivs and which are ours)

Blue Heron Breakfast by Barbara Whitt

BOOK CLUB QUESTIONS

1. The author reflects on migration and finding a sense of "home." How do these themes resonate with the author's personal journey and the wider narrative of the American Dream?

2. How does the author weave together the contrasting rhythms of farm life and the film industry? How do these two worlds influence each other in her narrative?

3. How does Muriel Murch's role as a mother, wife, and individual evolve throughout the book?

4. How does the village agricultural community shape the life experiences, development and world views of the family?

5. What does the book reveal about the environmental movements and agricultural practices in Marin County? How does the author connect these to broader social changes?

6. How does the book address the changing dynamics of small-town life, from farming traditions to the rise of the new environmental and social priorities? What insights does it offer into generational continuity and change?

7. The book blends journal entries, essays and storytelling. How does this structure affect your reading experience? Do you find it enhances or detracts from the themes explored?

8. The author frequently draws parallels between natural processes and creative endeavors. How do these connections deepen the book's central themes?

9. Which anecdote or character resonated most with you and why? How do they contribute to the overall narrative?

10. The book includes recipes and descriptions of farm life. How do these elements contribute to the memoir's tone and immersive quality? What lessons or inspirations can be drawn from the author's reflections on sustainable living and community resilience? How relevant are these lessons today?

Sibylline
PRESS

www.ingramcontent.com/pod-product-compliance
Lightning Source LLC
Chambersburg PA
CBHW030400130626
46549CB00004B/1577